Environmental Law in Action

Addressing Crime and Justice

Aishwarya

Foreworded by

Prof. (Dr) Nuzhat Parveen Khan

&

Prof. (Dr) Aditya Tomer

This book is dedicated to

My Father and Mother

With Love

Contents

1. THE EMERGENCE OF SUSTAINABLE DEVELOPMENT 1

I. The Emergence of the Term and its Necessity

II. Sustainable Development Goals

III. India's Involvement

IV. The Emergence of Sustainability in India

V. Challenges

VI. Strategies for Sustainable Development in India

VII. Affordable Housing

VIII. Critical Issues

IX. Government Measures

2. THE ENVIRONMENT, JUDICIAL INTERVENTION AND CONSTITUTIONAL PROVISIONS 15

I. Need for Environmental Laws

II. Tortious Liability

III. Strict Liability

IV. The Constitutional Aspects on Environmental Law

List of Acronyms

Anr	Another
CAMPA	Compensatory Afforestation Planning and Management Authority
CBD	Convention on Biological Diversity
CEC	Central Empowered Committee
CETPs	Common Effluent Treatment Plants
CIC	Central Information Commission
CNG	Compressed Natural Gas
CPCB	Central Pollution Control Board
CRZ	Coastal Regulation Zone
DPSP	Directive Principles of State Policy
EAC	Expert Appraisal Committee
EC	Environmental Clearance
EIA	Environmental Impact Assessment
EU	European Union
ICJ	International Court of Justice
IMF	International Monetary Fund
ITLOS	International Tribunal for the Law of the Sea
IUCN	International Union for Conservation of Nature and Natural Resources
MA	Miscellaneous Application

MDGs	**Millennium Development Goals**
MHRD	**Ministry of Human Resources Development**
MoEF	**Ministry of Environment and Forests**
MoEFCC	**Ministry of Environment, Forest and Climate Change**
NEAA	**National Environment Appellate Authority**
NEERI	**National Environmental Engineering Research Institute**
NGO	**Non-governmental Organisation**
NGT	**National Green Tribunal**
NPV	**Net Present Value**
OA	**Original Application**
OECD	**Organisation for Economic Cooperation and Development**
Ors	**Others**
PIL	**Public Interest Litigation**
RLEK	**Rural Litigation and Entitlement Kendra**
SDGs	**Sustainable Development Goals**
SPCB	**State Pollution Control Board**
ST	**Scheduled Tribes**
UNCED	**United Nations Conference on Environment and Development**
UNCTAD	**United Nations Council on Trade and Development**
UNEP	**United Nations Environment Programme**

UNFCCC	**United Nations Framework Convention on Climate Change**
WP	**Writ Petition**
WSSD	**WWWorld Summit on Sustainable Development**
WTO-DSB	**Dispute Resolution Body of the World Trade Organisation**

Foreword

In an age where the human footprint is more visible than ever, the urgency to confront environmental crimes has become a defining challenge of our time. The degradation of our planet's ecosystems through illegal logging, poaching, pollution, and unsustainable resource extraction is not only a threat to biodiversity but to human survival itself. Every forest felled, every river contaminated, and every species driven to extinction reverberates far beyond its immediate consequences, destabilizing entire communities, economies, and, ultimately, our future.

Environmental crimes, once perceived as peripheral offenses, now stand at the forefront of global legal debates. The sheer scale and impact of these crimes have forced nations to confront difficult questions: How can we effectively legislate against actions that threaten the very foundations of life on Earth? What role do national and international laws play in ensuring accountability and justice? And how can we balance economic development with the urgent need for environmental preservation?

This book aims to explore these pressing questions, offering insights into the complex interplay between law, policy, and environmental protection. It delves into the intricacies of environmental law highlighting successes, uncovering gaps, and proposing pathways forward. From landmark cases that set global precedents to grassroots movements that demand systemic change, the stories within these pages reveal the power and limitations of the legal system in addressing environmental degradation.

As we face the realities of climate change, diminishing resources, and increasing environmental conflicts, this book serves as both a guide and a call to action. It is a reminder that the law is not just a tool for punishment but a framework for building a more just and sustainable future.

The battle for the environment is not fought solely in the courtroom or the halls of government; it is waged in our collective consciousness. It challenges each of us—lawmakers, enforcers, citizens—to redefine our relationship with the natural world. The choices we make today will determine the health of our planet for generations to come.

India, a country of immense biodiversity and ecological richness, stands at a crucial juncture in its environmental history. From the majestic Himalayas to the lush Western Ghats, and from the expansive forests of the Northeast to the arid deserts of Rajasthan, India's natural heritage is both vast and vulnerable. However, as the nation continues to grow economically, it faces profound environmental challenges—challenges that are now met with increasing legal scrutiny.

Environmental crimes, including illegal mining, deforestation, pollution, and the exploitation of wildlife, pose significant threats not only to the country's ecosystems but also to its cultural and economic fabric. While India's environmental diversity is a source of pride, it is also at risk from rapid industrialization, unchecked urbanization, and the ever-growing demands of a burgeoning population. Against this backdrop, the role of environmental law in India becomes ever more critical.

India has a robust framework of environmental legislation, much of which was born out of the growing awareness of the need to protect its natural resources. Landmark laws such as the **Environment (Protection) Act, 1986**, the **Wildlife (Protection) Act, 1972**, the **Air (Prevention and Control of Pollution) Act, 1981**, and the **Water (Prevention and Control of Pollution) Act, 1974**, form the backbone of India's legal response to environmental issues. These laws reflect India's commitment to safeguarding its environment, balancing development with the need for conservation.

Yet, despite these laws, the gap between legislation and enforcement remains a persistent challenge. Judicial activism has often stepped in to fill this void, with the **Supreme Court of India** and the **National Green Tribunal (NGT)** playing pivotal roles in interpreting and enforcing environmental statutes. Their interventions have ranged from ordering the cleanup of polluted rivers to halting destructive mining operations, showcasing the law's potential as a powerful instrument of environmental protection.

However, the question remains: Are India's environmental laws equipped to deal with the scale and complexity of today's ecological crises? Can legal frameworks alone address issues as vast as climate change, habitat destruction, and pollution, or is a more integrated approach required?

This book seeks to explore these critical issues, providing a comprehensive examination of India's environmental legal landscape. It delves into the history of environmental legislation in the country, highlights key legal battles, and reflects on the successes and limitations of India's efforts to combat environmental crimes. By doing so, it hopes to contribute to the ongoing conversation about how best to preserve the nation's ecological wealth while ensuring sustainable development for its people.

In a country as vast and diverse as India, the need for strong environmental governance is more urgent than ever. This book serves as a reminder that environmental laws are not just technical instruments but moral commitments to future generations. The law must evolve in tandem with the pressing realities of environmental degradation, ensuring that the natural wonders of India are preserved for centuries to come.

This book explores the intricate intersections between environmental law, environmental crime, indigenous rights, sustainable development, and a comprehensive array of case laws. This book arrives at a critical juncture in human history, where the relationship between nature and legal systems is more important than ever. Environmental degradation, climate change, and the marginalization of indigenous communities are issues that no longer sit on the periphery of law and governance; they now demand the urgent attention of scholars, policymakers, and practitioners alike.

The environment has always been central to the existence of life on Earth, but it is only in recent decades that the field of environmental law has developed into a robust discipline capable of addressing the multitude of challenges facing the natural world. Environmental law is unique in that it seeks to balance competing interests: development versus conservation, human progress versus ecological sustainability, and the rights of present generations versus the rights of future generations. As this book astutely examines, these competing interests are at the heart of numerous legal disputes and debates worldwide, but particularly in India— a nation that represents both the promise and the peril of modern environmental governance.

One of the central themes of this book is the concept of Sustainable Development. The term has become something of a rallying cry for governments and international organizations around the globe, but what does it really mean? How can we ensure that development today does not compromise the ability of future generations to meet their own needs? The author deftly navigates these questions, unpacking the legal framework around sustainable development and discussing how this principle has been applied in environmental case law. In particular, the reader will find a detailed analysis of India's legal approach to sustainable development, including landmark cases such as Vellore Citizens Welfare Forum v. Union of India (1996) and the integration of international principles like the Precautionary Principle and the Polluter Pays Principle into Indian law.

The author also focuses on the role of environmental crime in exacerbating ecological degradation. Environmental crimes, ranging from illegal logging and wildlife poaching to industrial pollution and unlawful land use, are often overlooked in mainstream legal discourse. However, as the book elucidates, these crimes have far-reaching consequences, not only for the environment but for the vulnerable communities whose lives and livelihoods depend on it.

One of the most compelling sections of this book is its examination of indigenous rights in the context of environmental law. Indigenous communities have long been the stewards of their natural environments, maintaining sustainable practices that have allowed ecosystems to flourish for centuries. Yet, these very communities are often the first to suffer from environmental exploitation, whether through deforestation, mining, or water pollution. This book highlights the tension between state-led development projects and the rights of indigenous peoples, with a special focus on India's Adivasi communities. By exploring key legal battles—such as the Niyamgiri case, where the Dongria Kondh tribe successfully resisted a bauxite mining project on their sacred land—the author demonstrates how indigenous rights are both protected and contested within the framework of environmental law.

Case law, as a cornerstone of any legal system, plays a pivotal role in shaping the future of environmental protection. This book delves into some of the most significant environmental cases in India and around the world, analyzing how courts have responded to the complexities of environmental disputes. Cases like M.C. Mehta v. Union of India (1987), which introduced the principle of absolute liability for industries engaged in hazardous activities, and Subhash Kumar v. State of Bihar (1991), which established the right to a pollution-free environment under Article 21 of the Indian Constitution, have set important legal precedents. The author not only reviews these landmark judgments but also critically evaluates their implementation, addressing the gap between judicial rulings and on-the-ground realities.

In addition to case law, the book sheds light on the broader legal frameworks governing environmental protection in India, including constitutional provisions, statutory laws, and international treaties. The discussion on the National Green Tribunal (NGT) is particularly insightful, as the NGT has emerged as a critical institution for addressing environmental disputes in a timely and specialized manner. By comparing the NGT's functioning to environmental courts in other jurisdictions, the author offers valuable insights into the strengths and weaknesses of India's environmental legal apparatus.

Perhaps one of the greatest contributions of this volume is its ability to weave together disparate themes into a coherent narrative. Environmental law, environmental crime, indigenous rights, and sustainable development are often treated as separate areas of study, yet they are deeply interconnected. This book does an admirable job of highlighting these connections, showing how environmental degradation often goes hand-in-hand with the violation of human rights, particularly the rights of marginalized communities. It also makes a strong case for the need to rethink our legal and ethical approaches to the environment, advocating for a more holistic and inclusive form of environmental governance.

As you read through the chapters of this meticulously researched and thoughtfully crafted book, it becomes clear that it is not just a legal text but also a call to action. The challenges facing the environment and the people who depend on it are immense, but so too are the opportunities for legal innovation and reform. This book provides both a rich academic foundation and a practical guide for those who wish to engage with the critical legal issues surrounding the environment. It will undoubtedly serve as a vital resource for students, scholars, legal practitioners, policymakers, and activists alike. May this book inspire a deeper understanding of environmental crimes and a renewed commitment to using the law as a force for good in protecting the Earth.

Aishwarya deserve appreciation for putting together a volume that combines moral urgency and legal acuity of our planet earth.

September 2024

Prof.(Dr.) Nuzhat Parveen Khan
Professor and Former Dean Faculty of Law
Jamia Millia Islamia New Delhi

Foreword

In an era marked by an escalating environmental crisis, the importance of understanding the intricate relationship between environmental justice, legal frameworks, and the rights of indigenous communities cannot be overstated. This book, authored by Ms. Aishwarya, is a timely and insightful contribution to this discourse, shedding light on some of the most pressing challenges of our times.

It is with great pride and optimism that I introduce this timely and significant work, which dives deep into the nexus of environmental law, environmental crime, and tribal rights. In a world where the fragility of our ecosystems is increasingly apparent, and marginalized communities, especially indigenous groups, are facing heightened pressures, this book sheds light on the pressing issues that demand our immediate attention and action.

The environment, for centuries, has been the silent witness to humanities growth, industrialization, and development. However, it has also been a silent sufferer. With each step towards modernization, we have, inadvertently or otherwise, left behind traces of destruction. The natural world has borne the brunt of industrial progress, and in many cases, the most vulnerable communities especially indigenous tribes have suffered alongside. The intersection of environmental justice and the rights of these communities is not just a legal issue, but a human one. It speaks to the very core of how we, as a society, value life, culture, and the natural world around us.

This book embarks on a journey through the evolving landscape of environmental law in India, tracing the path from ancient traditions to modern-day legal frameworks. Aishwarya's work is not just an academic inquiry but also a heartfelt exploration into the stories of those who often go unheard—the indigenous communities whose lives are intricately tied to the environment. Their struggle against powerful corporate interests, especially in the face of exploitative mining practices, is not just a matter of legal dispute, but one of human dignity.

One of the most striking aspects of this work is its multidimensional approach. Aishwarya masterfully weaves together the historical, legal, and social facets of environmental crime and justice. She provides a historical context for environmental governance, tracing back to India's ancient practices of environmental protection, which were deeply rooted in sustainability and respect for nature. Her analysis of key events such as the Stockholm Declaration and the emergence of sustainable development add depth to the understanding of how global frameworks have shaped India's environmental policies.

At the heart of this exploration is the concept of environmental justice a notion that goes beyond mere legal compliance. It is about fairness, equity, and the recognition that those who contribute the least to environmental degradation often suffer its worst consequences. Indigenous communities, who have lived harmoniously with nature for centuries, are now facing existential threats from deforestation, mining, and other environmentally destructive practices. Aishwarya's work highlights these injustices and calls for a legal framework that not only protects the environment but also upholds the rights of these communities.

What I find particularly admirable about this book is the way it marries legal analysis with moral philosophy. The author does not shy away from questioning the ethical implications of our current environmental policies. She challenges the reader to think about the long-term consequences of environmental degradation, not just for the planet but for future generations. In doing so, she echoes the sentiment of global leaders who have long argued for a more sustainable and equitable world.

Furthermore, Aishwarya's deep understanding of the Constitutionality of India's environmental laws is commendable. Her chapter on the Wildlife Act and its alignment with constitutional provisions provides a nuanced analysis that is often lacking in other works on the subject. She brings to light the gaps in the legal system while offering constructive recommendations. Her passion for environmental justice is palpable throughout the book, and it is clear that this work is not just an academic pursuit for her but a personal mission.

In conclusion, this book is more than just a legal text. It is a call to action. It reminds us of the fragile balance between development and conservation and urges us to rethink our relationship with the environment. It implores lawmakers, corporations, and citizens alike to adopt a more compassionate and equitable approach to environmental governance. Aishwarya's work is a beacon of hope for those who believe in the power of law to bring about meaningful change. It is a must-read for anyone invested in the future of our planet and the rights of those who call it home.

I am confident that this book will serve as an invaluable resource for students, scholars, policymakers, and activists alike. It will not only enrich the academic discourse on environmental law but also inspire real-world change.

I extend my heartfelt congratulations to Aishwarya for her dedication, and I eagerly look forward

to see the positive impact her work will undoubtedly have on both the legal community and society at large.

September 2024

Prof. (Dr) Aditya Tomer,
Dean, School of Law,
Galgotias University.

Acknowledgements

Writing this book has been a deeply enriching journey, and it would not have been possible without the support and guidance of several important individuals. I am deeply grateful to the many people who have contributed to the completion of this book. First and foremost, I wish to express my heartfelt gratitude to my parents, whose unwavering support, encouragement, and love have been my constant source of strength. Their sacrifices, belief in my dreams, and endless motivation have made this journey possible. I dedicate this work to them.

I wish to extend my deepest gratitude to **Prof. Nuzhat Parveen Khan,** whose unwavering guidance and encouragement have been instrumental in shaping this book. Her insightful feedback, mentorship, and steadfast support throughout this journey have been invaluable. I am especially grateful to her for forwarding this book, believing in its potential, and providing the intellectual direction that helped me refine my ideas. This work would not have been possible without her inspiration and dedication to the pursuit of knowledge.

I extend my heartfelt gratitude to our respected Dean **Prof. (Dr) Aditya Tomar** for his support and invaluable guidance throughout the development of this book. Your willingness to endorse my work, coupled with your thoughtful advice, has not only been a source of encouragement but has also deepened my confidence in the importance of this research. I am sincerely thankful for your leadership and for creating an academic environment that nurtures growth and excellence. Your belief in both me and this project has been a constant source of inspiration during this journey.

I am also indebted to my colleagues and friends, whose camaraderie and intellectual exchange have enriched this research. Your constructive feedback, stimulating discussions, and unwavering support have been a source of inspiration. I am grateful for the countless hours you spent listening, advising, and offering your perspectives, which have been crucial in refining the ideas presented in this book.

This book would not have been possible without the support of each one of you. Thank you for being part of this journey and for contributing to the realization of this dream.

Introduction

The environment, encompassing all living and non-living things surrounding us, is integral to human survival and well-being. It provides essential resources such as air, water, food, and shelter, while also maintaining the delicate balance necessary for sustaining life on Earth. In recent decades, however, rapid industrialization, urbanization, and unregulated exploitation of natural resources have led to significant environmental degradation. This has resulted in air and water pollution, deforestation, loss of biodiversity, and climate change, posing severe threats to human health and the ecosystem.

In response to the growing environmental crisis, the need for a robust legal framework to protect the environment has become indispensable. Environmental law refers to the collection of legal principles, regulations, and policies aimed at safeguarding the environment from harmful human activities while promoting sustainable development. These laws not only regulate the use of natural resources but also ensure accountability for environmental harm, thus striking a balance between development and conservation.

In India, the recognition of the importance of environmental protection can be traced back to ancient times when nature was revered and protected through religious and cultural traditions. However, the formal codification of environmental laws began under colonial rule, particularly with the enactment of forest and wildlife laws. Post-independence, environmental concerns gained prominence, especially with the adoption of key constitutional provisions.

The Indian Constitution, under Article 48-A, directs the state to protect and improve the environment, while Article 51-A (g) makes it the duty of every citizen to safeguard the natural environment. Landmark legislation such as the Environment Protection Act, 1986, and the Forest Conservation Act, 1980, laid the foundation for India's modern environmental legal framework. These laws have been supplemented by judicial activism, particularly through public interest litigations (PILs) and the establishment of specialized bodies like the National Green Tribunal (NGT).

Despite the existence of these legal frameworks, challenges such as weak enforcement, corruption, and conflicts between development goals and environmental protection continue to impede their effectiveness. Nevertheless, environmental law in India remains a crucial tool in the fight against environmental degradation, reflecting the nation's commitment to achieving a sustainable and just future.

Chapter 1
The Emergence of Sustainable Development

I. The Emergence of the Term and its Necessity

In 1972, the United Nations Conference on the Human Environment took place in Stockholm which highlighted the concerns for preventing pollution and enhancing biodiversity and environment to ensure the rights of humans to a healthy and progressive environment.

In 1987, the United Nations World Commission on Environment and Development issued the Brundtland Report which emphasized three fundamental components of sustainable development: environmental protection, economic growth and social equity.

In 1992 Rio de Janeiro Conference, it marked the first international attempt to draw up action plans and strategies for moving towards a more sustainable pattern of development.

The term sustainable development was defined as a way of development where the needs of the present are met without compromising the ability of future generations to meet their own needs. It was coined by Doctor Gro Harlem in the Brundtland Report. The concept of needs in the definition refers to the essential needs of the world's poor which should be given ultimate priority. There also needs to be an idea of limitation imposed on the environment's ability to be able to meet present and future needs.

The necessity of sustainable development and its implementation was realized when imperative changes in the functioning and effects of environment were noticed. The changes followed by disasters acted as an alarm to what the future could behold, the understanding of which led to the foundation of concept of sustainable development and living. It was argued that if humans keep acting independently towards pursuing their individual interests then it won't be long before all the resources exhaust due to over exploitation. It was thereby felt that mankind needed to change its ways and means and diverge to a sustainable development track.

II. Sustainable Development Goals

Sustainable development goals were adopted in 2015 by all member nations of the United Nations as a universal action to end poverty and pollution, thereby protecting the planet and providing peace and prosperity to everybody by the advent of 2030. They represent the post 2015 development agenda and are a set of 17 goals consisting of 169 targets globally set to be the blueprint towards a better and more sustainable future for all.

The three primary objectives of sustainable development goals are:

- Economic growth.

- Environmental protection.

- Social inclusion.

The sustainable development goals have succeeded over millennial development goals in content and applicability. The previous goals were being criticized for being too narrow in description and superficial in implementation. The millennial development goals focused more on world development through relations between countries and their support towards development of other countries. The newly drafted sustainable development goals were far wider in context and provided a much more inclusive perspective and framework towards development without depending on the relation between the countries. They were more globally applicable and were created by the largest United Nations program thereby providing a firm foundation.

The sustainable development goals are:

1. No Poverty: By 2030, eradicate extreme poverty for all people everywhere.

2. Zero Hunger: End hunger, achieve food security and improved nutrition by 2030.

3. Good Health and Well-being: Ensure healthy lives and promote well-being for all at all ages by 2030.

4. Quality Education: Ensure that all girls and boys complete free, equitable and quality primary and secondary education by 2030.

5. Gender Equality: To achieve gender equality and empower all women and girls.

6. Clean Water and Sanitation: Ensure availability and sustainable management of water and sanitation for all by 2030.

7. Affordable and Clean Energy: Ensure access to affordable, reliable, sustainable and modern energy for all by 2030.

8. Decent Work and Economic Growth: Promote sustained, inclusive and sustainable economic growth.

9. Industry, Innovation and Infrastructure: Build resilient infrastructure, promote inclusive and sustainable industrialization and foster innovation by 2030.

10. Reduced Inequality: Reduce inequality within and among countries by 2030.

11. Sustainable Cities and Communities: Make cities and human settlements inclusive, safe, resilient and sustainable.

12. Responsible Consumption and Production: Ensure sustainable consumption and production patterns.

13. Climate Action: Take urgent action to combat climate change and its impacts.

14. Life below Water: Conserve and sustainably use the oceans, seas and marine resources for sustainable development.

15. Life on Land: Protect, restore and promote sustainable use of terrestrial ecosystems, combat desertification and halt biodiversity loss.

16. Peace, Justice and Strong Institutions: Promote peaceful and inclusive societies for sustainable development; provide access to justice for all.

17. Partnerships to achieve goals: Strengthen the means of implementation and revitalize the global partnership for sustainable development.

III. India's Involvement

India has a major contribution in the framing of the sustainable development goals. It was the only country to argue for initiation and adoption of nationally determined contributions to measure and map the progress of sustainable development goals. India has also demonstrated bold commitment to provide funding to the United Nations trust for the institution of SDGs. It was one of the few countries to begin effective planning for the achievement of SDGs even before their final crystallization. India became one of the foremost countries to participate in Voluntary National Reviews (VNRs) where various surveys are used to measure and graph the progress of ascertained goals, thereby promoting the inculcation of the sustainable development goals. India's role is a long lineage based on three parameters- ideation, diplomacy and institutional. The country has been largely associated with formulation and implementation of international norms which have also been accepted by all member nations with complete harmony. In diplomacy, India has worked with the G77 nations to help them collaborate better with the norms put forth and has worked towards bringing the nations to consensus agreements reaping benefits for all. Institutionally, India's endeavor has always been to strengthen the purview and aim of the United Nations in economic, political and environmental matters. Even the agreements not pertaining to the UN have been persuaded to follow similar principles and guidelines by active participation and promotion by India.

IV. The Emergence of Sustainability in India

The doctrine of sustainable development in India was introduced by the case of Vellore Citizen Welfare Forum v. Union of India. It was held in this case that precautionary principle and polluter pays principle are the basis of sustainability. In the case of Narmada Bachao v. Union of India[1], it was stated that development should be of the extent that can be sustained by nature with no or little mitigation. On similar lines it was held, in the case of Indian Council for Enviro Legal Action v. Union of India[2], that while economic development should not be done at the cost of ecological destruction, the same should not be hampering economic development. It was stated that economic and ecological developments should be well balanced with effectiveness of both intact.

Related laws and implementations in India

There are several laws which have been passed which include

- The Water (Prevention and Control of Pollution) Act of 1974

- The Forest (Conservation) Act of 1980

- The Air (Prevention and Control of Pollution) Act of 1981

- The Environment (Protection) Act of 1986

National Green Tribunal: The legislature enacted The National Green Tribunal Act in 2010 after attending all major environmental conferences around the world. The tribunal aims at effective and quick disposal of cases involving multi corporal issues related to the environment. NGT is empowered to hear all matters related to environment and has furthered the crusade of environment protection aiming for better and effective implementation of sustainable development goals. The tribunal is not bound by Code of Civil Procedure 1908, instead is supposed to follow the principles of natural justice. In the case of Prafulla Samantray v. Union of India[3], the tribunal ordered suspension of the POSCO (South Korean steel-making company) steel plant in Odisha with the opinion that though there is need for industrial development, it should be within the parameters of sustainable development and should keep in check all related environmental concerns.

---

1. Narmada Bachao Andolan v. Union of India (2000) 10 SCC 664

2 Indian Council for Enviro-legal Action v. Union of India (1996) 3 SCC

3 Prafulla Samantray v. Union of India, (2013) 12 SCC 792

The phrase of the present government "Sbka Saath Sbka Vikas" which translates to 'collective effort, inclusive development' is being stated as the countries national development agenda. Several of the government's programs would directly contribute to advancement of the SDG agenda. These include Swachh Bharat mission, Beti Bacho Beti Padhao, Pradhan Mantri Awas Yojana, Smart Cities, Pradhan Mantri Jan Dhan Yojana, Deen Dayal Upadhyay Gram Jyoti Yojana and Pradhan Mantri Ujjwala Yojana, among others4.

The Namami Gange Mission: This integrated conservation mission was introduced in 2014 with the twin objective of rejuvenation and preservation of the national river ganga. The mission encompasses the development and maintenance of sewage treatment infrastructure and also factory effluents handling. It also takes into account public awareness, effective afforestation and riverfront development and cleaning procedures5.

National Clean Air Programme in 2019: India formally joined the climate and clean air coalition for effective implementation of the national clean air programme which is a comprehensive plan to reduce air pollution, keep it in check and simultaneously improve the Air Quality Index. This was done in consideration to the recent massive dropping of the quality of air in the northern region of the country.[6]

Nature has offered us with renewable and nonrenewable resources that have made our lives quite convenient and continue to help us with our advancement in technology. More and more resources are being used up to meet the increasing demands of the growing population which will soon result in depletion of these resources. Not only will the present population suffer due to this lack of availability of resources but also, it will compromise the needs of the future generations as they would be deprived of the natural resources which

---

4.   Ministry of External Affairs. (2019). India and Sustainable Development Goals: Achievements and way forward. *Government of India.*

5.   Ministry of Jal Shakti. (2014). Namami Gange Mission: Rejuvenation and preservation of the Ganga. *Government of India.*

6.   Ministry of Environment, Forest and Climate Change. (2019). National Clean Air Programme (NCAP): A comprehensive plan for air quality improvement. *Government of India.*

even they have a right to use. To secure the present and future generations, the concept of sustainable development was introduced which satisfied the needs of the present without compromising the capacity of the people in future, guaranteeing a balance between economic growth, protection of the environment and social well-being. This development focused on improving the global quality of life which meant bringing about such changes in the environment that could enhance the economic, social, cultural and political conditions of the people so that both the rights of the people as well as the environment is safeguarded.

The developing countries like India have to emphasize more on this concept as all their resources are being used to cater to the needs of the growing population and yet due to an imbalance in the economic growth, the majority part of this population does not have a proper house to live in. The country needed a plan that could provide affordable homes for the low-income population and also ensure that the principles of sustainable development are upheld while constructing and building such homes. This article discusses how by bringing both sustainable development and affordable housing, the problems of many homeless people could be solved without causing any harm to the environment.

V. Challenges

There are many hurdles on the path leading to complete sustainable development of the world. These hurdles are very much visible to all the people however, many of them choose to ignore them. The major challenge for sustainable development is to fulfill its goals keeping in mind that not all the people are supportive of its ways and measures. The main challenges faced are as follows-

- The major challenge for sustainable development is population growth. Increase in the population indicates an increase in the demands of the people. Every individual requires a house, the basic facilities of food and water, electricity, heavy appliances, a car, etc. which are common nowadays to be found in almost every household. They are habitual of the technologies that they use and are not ready to compromise for the sake of the environment. Thus, sustainable development has to be achieved in such a way that their present needs are fulfilled without straining the needs of future generations.

- The developing countries, for example, India, are dependent on the resources to cope up with the growing demands of its population and also to develop its nation from a global point of view as developing countries are already behind in many things. There is a lack of financial resources to carry out plans for sustainable development efficiently. India is struck with poverty for a long time now. The government does not have many job opportunities for everyone or enough resources to spend on individuals as well as maintain its international relations. Without any kind of financial aid, it is difficult to achieve sustainable development in the country.

- Inequality is another challenge faced by people who want to promote sustainable development. While there is a section of the society that enjoys all the luxuries of food, drinking water and housing, there are people who are suffering from undernourishment. Even so, food production is exhausting the resources available to us through nature.

- Consumption of Energy is another hurdle. There are many industries and other facilities that are using all forms of energy for their convenience. A reliable and sustainable source of energy is required so that no harm is done to the environment.

VI. Strategies for Sustainable Development in India

India seems to be facing all the challenges that are stopping it from achieving the goal of a sustainable environment. There are certain strategies that are devised to manage and utilize the resources in a proper way to ensure sustainable development in the country. These strategies are as follows-

- Input Efficient Technology should be used in industries and other facilities to reduce the exploitation of resources.

- Eco-friendly fuels like Compressed Natural Gas (CNG) should be used in place of petrol and diesel to reduce the effect of greenhouse gases from the earth's atmosphere. The government should also advocate the use of renewable sources of energy like wind and solar energy. Though the process is expensive and difficult yet, it is necessary to make use of this energy now to safeguard the non-renewable resources from depleting.

- Special sustainable designs should be used for construction purposes. More recycling of waste products should be promoted so that the resources are not blindly exploited.

- The *State Action Plans on Climate Change (SAPCC)* – They aim to create institutional capacities and implement sectoral activities to address climate change. These plans are focused on adaptation with mitigation as a co-benefit in sectors such as water, agriculture, tourism, forestry, transport, habitat and energy.

VII. Affordable Housing

India has a huge population, yet there is a lack of available housing options in the country. Due to limited income and minimal access to home finance for those borrowers who have a low income, millions of people currently live in cramped, poorly constructed houses and some even live in slum areas where they do not even have a proper roof to live under. They lack access to a clean and healthy environment with no basic amenities such as clean water, sewage, waste management or electricity is provided to them. It is known that sustainable development aims for quality life among individuals and it looks after the health and well- being of people. Thus, the concept of 'Affordable Housing' is a part of sustainable development to provide better housing facilities to that section of the population that cannot afford proper homes to live in. It refers to housing units that are affordable for the low-income people and the economically weaker sections of the society staying in urban areas.

VIII. Critical Issues

Provision of affordable housing to the low-income population does fulfill one of the goals of sustainable development to ensure the health and well-being of individuals. However, this sector faces a few critical issues. They are as follows-

- There is a scarcity of land for construction of affordable housing. The high population density, rapid urbanization and improper regulations have led to the shortage of land parcels available for development. Poorly planned settlements like slums are spread over large areas leaving no space for housing projects.

- The costs of both land and construction have increased with the expenses of construction material and labour. A project like affordable housing needs financial aids to complete its target.

- Clearance of project sanctions takes many years as it passes through almost forty departments. No clear laws or regulations are framed for the project like by-laws, rules for floor space index and zoning.

- There are title issues that are raised whenever land is finalized. Problems of registration, court decrees, filing agreements and transactions are faced as it is a long process.

IX. Government Measures

- The government set 2022 as the target year to achieve housing for all in its initiative of the Pradhan Mantri Awas Yojana (PMAY) which comprises affordable housing for both the urban poor and the rural poor. The scheme gives financial assistance to the States and Union Territories to support housing requirements of the urban poor and the rural poor, focusing on the lower-income groups.[7]

- The government has also increased the time for the completion of the projects from three to five years and reduced the tenure for long-term capital gains for affordable housing from three to two years.

- The developers are provided with incentives including subsidies, tax benefits and institutional funding.

- The Goods and Services Tax (GST) Council has reduced tax rates for affordable housing from eight per cent to just one per cent.

---

7. Ministry of Housing and Urban Affairs. (n.d.). *Pradhan Mantri Awas Yojana (PMAY): Housing for All by 2022*. Government of India

- The Reserve Bank of India is also ready to give loans to affordable housing under priority sector lending.

Today, we see the increased frequency of natural disasters worldwide which have been linked to climate change. Various reports provide more and more evidence that human activities are at the origin of the greenhouse effect.

The question that comes to our mind is how to manage the human activities sustainably without impacting the climate. The basic control is on balancing the activities/thought processes to meet the requirements of all five senses and the activities towards giving out to the society through continuous monitoring of inward development (spiritualism).

Sustainable Development is the "development that meets the needs of the present without compromising the ability of future generations to meet their own needs".

The sustainability movement has nonetheless gained traction because of the evident inefficiency of our current products and production processes.

Because of the growing societal concerns viz; negative social and environmental impact of communication technologies, businesses are under strong pressure to measure their impacts on the natural and social environment and to engage in triple bottom line reporting to account for the energy and other resources they use, and the resulting footprint they leave behind.

Employees need to take pride in their work and need to believe their companies operate in a prudent and responsible manner and care about employee health and safety. Concerning the planet, aligning sustainability goals with employees (people) and market incentives (profit) can be difficult. That is, profit people and planet are not that easily balanced.

People can speak up, but planet cannot defend itself except that planet brings in natural disasters when planet can't defend itself. And, this natural disaster brings pain to a section of people getting impacted while others still not concerned till they themselves are impacted, which is already late.

Hence, it is better both for people and planet to think beyond profit. That is where spiritualism balancing with materialism helps in developing the mindset of the people.

Porter (1991) argued: "The conflict between environmental protection and economic competitiveness is a false dichotomy based on a narrow view of the sources of prosperity and a static view of competition"8.

We see natural disasters happening in recent times in more frequent interval around the world. One recent example is that of the flood situation, happened almost after 100 years in Chennai.

People can speak up loudly and clearly while defending themselves, when injustice is meted out to them either by corporate or by the political system of the place the same people belong to. But, the planet can't defend itself on its own, when it is impacted by environmental pollution, climate change. However, nature tries to balance out this impact by repeated occurrence of natural disasters plundering people's lives, economy and wealth.

In this backdrop, the responsibility of the government, society and the corporate sector in managing their information systems, standards, procedures, laws, operating instructions on day to day operations is the need of the hour. Any decision at any level in the corporate sector, government, society should naturally and properly balance concerns of economic as well as environmental sustainability, natural and social.

A stable (i.e. sustainable) stool requires at least three legs. A first leg is tangible top management (Corporate, Government, Local administrative body) commitment on clear operational strategy. Second leg, of course, is the execution plan (e.g. developing systems, processes, procedures and standards) of sustainable strategy, and, third leg is the individual who needs to carry the sustainability in his/her heart and mind.

At the same time, new innovations like, thermal power, atomic plant and so on without any sufficient natural assurance pose another danger to the situations, the aftereffect of which results in issues like global warming, climate

---

8. Porter, M. E. (1991). *America's green strategy. Scientific American*, 264(4), 168

change, acid rain, etc. Moreover, according to pattern of Indian legislature to make a number of legislations as opposed to addressing the reason for failure and disappointment, and passing new bills consistently is just like 'old wine in new bottle'. Therefore, there arises a requirement for a comprehensive analysis of the protection of the environment. In recent years, there has been a sustained focus on the role played by the higher judiciary in devising and monitoring the implementation of measures for pollution control, conservation of forests and wildlife protection.

Many of these judicial interventions have been triggered by the persistent incoherence in policy-making as well as the lack of capacity-building amongst the executive agencies. Devices such as Public Interest Litigation (PIL) have been prominently relied upon to tackle environmental problems, and this approach has its supporters as well as critics.

Chapter 2

The Environment, Judicial Intervention And Constitutional Provisions

The word "environment" relates to surroundings. It includes virtually everything. It can be can defined as anything which may be treated as covering the physical surroundings that are common to all of us, including air, space, land, water, plants and wildlife. According to the Webster Dictionary, it is defined as the "Aggregate of all the external condition and influences affecting the life and development of an organism.

The Environment (Protection) Act, 1986, under section 2(a) environment[9] "includes water, air and land and the inter- relationship which exists among and between water, air and land, and human beings, other living creatures, plants, micro-organism and property." Thus, after analyzing all the definitions, the basic idea that can be concluded is that environment means the surroundings in which we live and is essential for our life.

I. Need for Environmental Laws

Today we are living in nuclear arena. No one can overlook the harm caused to the environment by the nuclear bombs, dropped by airplanes belonging to the United States on the Japanese urban communities of Hiroshima and Nagasaki amid the last phases of World War II in 1945. Day to day innovation and advancement of technology, apart from development additionally expands the

---

9. The Environment (Protection) Act, 1986, Section 2(a). Ministry of Environment and Forests

risk to human life. Accordingly, there arises an intense and an acute need of the law to keep pace with the need of the society along with individuals. So now the question of environmental protection is a matter of worldwide concern, it is not confined to any country or territory.

Judicial remedies for environment pollution.

The remedies available in India for environmental protection comprise of tortious as well as statutory law remedies. The tortious remedies available are trespass, nuisance, strict liability and negligence. The statutory remedies incorporate: Citizen's suit, e.g.

- an activity brought under Section 19 of the Environmental (Protection) Act, 1986,[10]

- an activity under sec. 133, Criminal Procedure Code, 1973[11].and

- and activity brought under the section 268 for open irritation, under Indian Penal Code,1860[12]

Apart from this, a writ petition can be filed under Article 32 in the Supreme Court of India[13] or under Article 226 in the High Court[14].

II. Tortious Liability

The Indian judiciary has developed the following tortious remedies:

- **Damage**

    In the recent case of *Shriram Gas Leak*[15], involving a leakage of Oleum gas which resulted in substantial environmental harm to the citizens of Delhi, the Apex court held that the quantum of damages awarded

---

10. The Environment (Protection) Act, 1986, Section 19. Ministry of Environment and Forests
11. The Code of Criminal Procedure, 1973, Section 133
12. The Indian Penal Code, 1860, Section 268
13. The Constitution of India, 1950, Article 32
14. The Constitution of India, 1950, Article 226
15. M.C. Mehta v. Union of India, (1987) 1 SCC 395

must be proportionate to the capacity and magnitude of the polluter to pay. However, the Apex Court has deviated from this test in the *Bhopal Gas Tragedy*.

- **Injunction**

  The purpose of injunction is to prevent continuous wrong. The grant of perpetual injunction is governed by Sec.37 to 42 of the Specific Relief Act, 1963.[16]

- **Nuisance**

  Nuisance means the act which creates hindrance to the enjoyment of the person in form of smell, air, noise, etc.

  According to Stephen, nuisance is anything done to hurt or annoyance of lands, tenements of another and not amounting to trespass.

Nuisance can be divided into two categories

1. Private Nuisance – It is a substantial and unreasonable interference with the use and enjoyment of one's land.

2. Public Nuisance – It is an unreasonable interference with a general right of the public

Trespass

It means intentional or negligent direct interference with personal or proprietary rights without lawful excuses.

The two important requirements for trespass are:

1. There must be an intentional or negligent interference with personal or proprietary rights.

2. The interference with the personal or proprietary rights must be direct rather than consequential.

---

16. The Specific Relief Act, 1963, Sections 37-42

Negligence

It connotes failure to exercise the care that a reasonably prudent person would exercise in like circumstances.

III. Strict Liability

The rule enunciated in **_Rylands v. Fletcher_** [17] by Blackburn J. is that the person who for his own purpose brings on his land and collects and keeps there anything likely to be a mischief, if it escapes, must keep it as its peril, and if he does not do so is prima facie even though, he will be answerable for all the damage which is the natural consequence of its escape. The doctrine of strict liability has considerable utility in environmental pollution cases especially cases dealing with the harm caused by the leakage of hazardous substances.

Some remarkable principles and doctrines propounded by the Indian judiciary

- **Doctrine of Absolute Liability**

  THE BHOPAL CASE: *Union Carbide Corporation v. Union Of India* [18]

  In this case, the court held that, where an enterprise is occupied with an inherently dangerous or a hazardous activity and harm results to anybody by virtue of a mishap in the operation of such dangerous or naturally unsafe movement coming about, for instance, in getaway of poisonous gas, the enterprise is strictly and completely obligated to repay every one of the individuals who are influenced by the accident and such risk is not subject to any exemptions. Accordingly, Supreme Court created another trend of Absolute Liability without any exemption.

---

17   Rylands v. Fletcher (1868) UKHL 1, [1868] LR 3 HL 330.

18   Union Carbide Corporation v. Union of India, (1991) 4 SCC 584

- ## Polluter Pays Principles

"If anyone intentionally spoils the water of another ... let him not only pay damages, but purify the stream or cistern which contains the water..." – Plato

Polluter Pays Principle has become a very popular concept lately. 'If you make a mess, it's your duty to clean it up '- this is the fundamental basis of this slogan. It should be mentioned that in environment law, the 'polluter pays principle' does not allude to "fault." Instead, it supports a remedial methodology which is concerned with repairing natural harm. It's a rule in international environmental law where the polluting party pays for the harm or damage done to the natural environment.

*Vellore Citizen's Welfare Forum v. Union of India*19 The Supreme Court has declared that the polluter pays principle is an essential feature of the sustainable development.

- ## Precautionary Principle

The Supreme Court of India, in Vellore Citizens Forum Case, developed the following three concepts for the precautionary principle:

Environmental measures must anticipate, prevent and attack the causes of environmental degradation

Lack of scientific certainty should not be used as a reason for postponing measures

Onus of proof is on the actor to show that his action is benign.

- ## Public Trust Doctrine

The Public Trust Doctrine primarily rests on the principle that certain resources like air, water, sea and the forests have such a great importance to people as a whole that it would be wholly unjustified to make them a subject of private ownership.

---

19. Vellore Citizens' Welfare Forum v. Union of India, (1996) 5 SCC 647

M.C.Mehta v. Kamal Nath and Others[20]

The public trust doctrine, as discussed by court in this judgment is a part of the law of the land.

• **Doctrine Of Sustainable Development**

The World commission on Environment and Development (WCED) in its report prominently known as the 'Brundtland Report' named after the Chairman of the Commission Ms. GH Brundtland highlights the concept of sustainable development. As per Brundtland Report, Sustainable development signifies" development that meets the needs of the present without compromising the ability of the future generations to meet their own needs". There is a need for the courts to strike a balance between development and environment.[21]

Rural Litigation and Entitlement Kendra v. State of UP[22]

The court for the first time dealt with the issue relating to the environment and development; and held that, it is always to be remembered that these are the permanent assets of mankind and or not intended to be exhausted in one generation.

Vellore Citizen's Welfare Forum[23]

In this case, the Supreme Court observed that sustainable development has come to be accepted as a viable concept to eradicate poverty and improve the quality of human life while living within the carrying capacity of the supporting eco- system.

---

20. M.C. Mehta v. Kamal Nath and Others, (1997) 1 SCC 388
21. World Commission on Environment and Development (WCED). (1987). *Our Common Future* (Brundtland Report). Oxford University Press. Quote: "Development that meets the needs of the present without compromising the ability of the future generations to meet their own needs."
22. Rural Litigation and Entitlement Kendra v. State of Uttar Pradesh, 1985 AIR 652, 1985 SCR (3) 169
23. Vellore Citizens' Welfare Forum v. Union of India, (1996) 5 SCC 647.

IV. The Constitutional Aspects on Environmental Law

The Indian Constitution is amongst the few in the world that contains specific provisions on environment protection. The chapters directive principles of state policy and the fundamental duties are explicitly enunciated the nation commitment to protect and improve the environment. It was the first time when responsibility of protection of the environment imposed upon the states through Constitution (Forty Second Amendment) Act, 1976.

Article 48-A- the provision reads as follows: "The State shall endeavor to protect and improve the environment and to safeguard the forest and wildlife of the country." The Amendment also inserted Part VI-A (Fundamental duty) in the Constitution.[24]

Article 51-A (g) "It shall be duty of every citizen of India to protect and improve the natural environment including forests, lakes, and wildlife and to have compassion for living creature."[25]

In *Sachidanand Pandey* v. *State of West Bengal*[26], the Supreme Court observed "whenever a problem of ecology is brought before the court, the court is bound to bear in mind Article 48-

A and Article 51-A (g).

V. Environmental Protection: the Judicial Approach

There are numbers of the following judgments which clearly highlight the active role of judiciary in environmental protection these are follows:

---

24. The Constitution of India, 1950, Article 48-A
25. The Constitution of India, 1950, Article 51-A(g)
26. Sachidanand Pandey v. State of West Bengal, (1987) 2 SCC 295

A) The Right To A Wholesome Environment

Charan Lal Sahu Case[27]

The Supreme Court in this case said, the right to life guaranteed by Article 21 of the Constitution includes the right to a wholesome environment.

Damodhar Rao v. S. 0. Municipal Corporation Hyderabad[28]

The Court resorted to the Constitutional mandates under Articles 48A and 51A(g) to support this reasoning and went to the extent of stating that environmental pollution would be a violation of the fundamental right to life and personal liberty as enshrined in **Article 21** of the Constitution.

B) Public Nuisance: The Judicial Response

Ratlam Municipal Council v. Vardhichand[29]

The judgment of the Supreme Court in instant case is a land mark in the history of judicial activism in upholding the social justice component of the rule of law by fixing liability on statutory authorities to discharge their legal obligation to the people in abating public nuisance and making the environmental pollution free even if there is a budgetary constraints., **J. Krishna Iyer** observed that," social justice is due to and therefore the people must be able to trigger off the jurisdiction vested for their benefit to any public functioning." Thus he recognized PIL as a Constitutional obligation of the courts.

C) Judicial Relief Encompasses Compensation To Victims

Delhi gas leak case: *M.C. Mehta v. Union of India.*[30]

In instant case, the Supreme Court laid down two important principles of law:

---

27. Charan Lal Sahu v. Union of India, (1990) 1 SCC 613.
28. Damodhar Rao v. S.O. Municipal Corporation, Hyderabad, AIR 1987 AP 171
29. Ratlam Municipal Council v. Vardhichand, (1980) 4 SCC 162.
30. M.C. Mehta v. Union of India, (1987) 1 SCC 395.

1. The power of the Supreme Court to grant remedial relief for a proved infringement of a fundamental right (in case if Article21) includes the power to award compensation.

2. The judgment opened a new frontier in the Indian jurisprudence by introducing a new "no fault" liability standard (absolute liability) for industries engaged in hazardous activities which has brought about radical changes in the liability and compensation laws in India. The new standard makes hazardous industries absolutely liable from the harm resulting from its activities.

D) Fundamental Right to Water

The fundamental right to water has evolved in India, not through legislative action but through judicial interpretation. In ***Narmada Bachao Andolan v. Union of India and Ors.***[31], the Supreme Court of India upheld that "Water is the basic need for the survival of human beings and is part of the right to life and human rights as enshrined in Article 21 of the Constitution of India, and the right to healthy environment and to sustainable development are fundamental human rights implicit in the right to life.

VI. Public Awareness

In India, media is the fourth pillar of the popular government. It plays an exceptionally essential and compelling part in the general improvement of the country. The effect of media can be seen in the different trials directed by it just by publishing them in their media. Accordingly, the issue of environmental pollution can be checked by making mindfulness in the general population, in which media's part is extremely critical. The compelling agency of correspondence not just influences the mind of the individuals but is also capable of developing thoughts and desirable attitudes of the people for protecting environment.

---

31. Narmada Bachao Andolan v. Union of India (2000) 10 SCC 664

Regular Inspection

There is a requirement for a standard review apparatus, which can inspect and examine periodically every one of those exercises which are threatening the environment. This would be a successful step towards environment protection, since prevention is better than cure.

There is no means for any law, unless it's an effective and successful implementation, and for effective implementation, public awareness is a crucial condition. Therefore, it is essential that there ought to be proper awareness. This contention is additionally maintained by the Apex Court in the instance of ***M.C. Mehta v. Union of India***[32]. In this case, Court directed the Union Government was obliged to issue directions to all the State governments and the union territories to enforce through authorities as a condition for license on all cinema halls, to obligatory display free of expense no less than two slides/messages on environment amid each show. Moreover, Law Commission of India in its 186th report made a proposal for the constitution of the environment court. Hence, there is an urgent need to strengthen the hands of judiciary by making separate environmental courts, with a professional judge to manage the environment cases/criminal acts, so that the judiciary can perform its part more viably.

---

32. M.C. Mehta v. Union of India, (1992) 3 SCC 256

Chapter 3

Stockholm Declaration

The United Nations Conference on the Human Environment- In 1968-1969, the General Assembly, by Resolutions 2398 and 2581 decided to conduct the conference. The Stockholm Convention was held in Sweden from June 5-16, 1972. The object behind this convention was to "create a basis for comprehensive consideration within the United Nations of the problems of the human environment," and to "focus the attention of Governments and public opinion in various countries on the importance of the problem." This convention led UNEP to coordinate global action for the protection and preservation of the environment in December 1972.

Many issues were resolved before the actual conference by the countries to limit the number of issues during the convention. This was primarily done by the conference secretariat. The conference secretariat headed by Mr. Maurice F. Strong planned the conference meticulously.[33]

The convention adopted the following:

1. A basic declaration containing a set of common principles to aid the people in protecting and conserving the environment.

2. A detailed resolution for financial and institutional arrangements for environmental protection.

3. An action plan containing 109 recommendations. This aims to identify and quantify the environmental problems, warn about any crisis, and to adopt supporting measures, by establishing an Earth watch.

---

33. United Nations Conference on the Human Environment. (1972). *Proceedings of the United Nations Conference on the Human Environment.* United Nations

At the end of the convention 26 principles were adopted and declared by the participating states. This is known as the Magna Carta of the human environment.

I. Significance

The declaration is divided into 2 parts. The first part contains seven truths about man and his connection with the environment. It also contains general observations, such as those men are both creators and molders of their environment. The protection of the environment is a pressing issue. It is the desire of the citizens of all the nations and the responsibility of all the governments to protect and preserve the environment. The second part contains 26 principles which form the basis of the international policy for the protection and preservation of the environment.

II. Principles of the Stockholm Declaration

The 26 principles[34] or the Magna Carta on the human environment are dealt with in great detail. For better understanding, the principles are grouped on their applicability and enforceability. They are as follows:

Human-centric (Principles 1 and 15)

Principle 1: Rights and Responsibilities for protecting the environment – Humans have the right to use and enjoy nature. The right to enjoy nature is not unfettered; it is coextensive with the duty to protect it. Art. 21 of the constitution also safeguard the fundamental right of a healthy environment. This principle also explicitly bars discriminatory laws.

Principle 15: Human settlement and Urbanization – Planned settlements and urbanization are required. They reduce the adverse effects on the environment. The goal is to secure maximum benefits for all through planning. All discriminatory plans are also barred.

Sustainable development (Principles 2, 3, 4, 5, 13 and 14)

---

34. United Nations Conference on the Human Environment, Stockholm Declaration, 1972

Principle 2: Duty to protect natural resources – Natural resources is limited. We must use natural resources carefully. Preservation of resources depends on effective planning and management.

Principle 3: Duty to preserve renewable resources – Although renewable resources are not depletable, their preservation is necessary for their quality.

Principle 4: Wildlife Conservation – A combination of factors is responsible for endangering wildlife. Humans have a special responsibility for protecting wildlife. The inclusion of conservation of wildlife in economic planning leads to sustainable development.

Principle 5: Duty to preserve non-renewable resources – Non-renewable resources are exhaustible. They are valuable resources. Exercising care and caution is necessary to prevent them from depletion

Principle 13: Rational Management of Resources – States should adopt rational methods to manage the resources and to improve the environment. An integrated and coordinated approach is preferable.

Principle 14: Rational Planning – Conflicts between development and conservation are reconciled with rational planning. Development and conservation must go hand in hand.

Reflection on customary international law position (Principle 21)

States have the absolute authority to use natural resources according to their policies. However, their policies shouldn't violate the principles of international law and cause damage to other states outside its jurisdiction.

Preventive actions (Principles 6, 7, 8 and 18)

Principle 6: Management of pollution – Pollution is harmful to the environment. Discharging toxins and other substances in large quantities are harmful to the ecosystem. Both the citizens and the states should play an active role in reducing the dumping of harmful substances.

Principle 7: Management of sea pollution – The states should reduce sea pollution by taking necessary steps to prevent substances hazardous to human health, marine life, and the legitimate uses of seas.

Principle 8: Social and Economic development – The improvement of social and economic conditions is necessary for a better living and working environment. Improvements shouldn't affect the environment in any way.

Principle 18: Application of science – Science and technology are indispensable in today's life. They are used in almost every industry. Science and technology are also applicable to the conservation of the environment. It is useful for identifying and controlling environmental risks. They are useful for finding solutions for environmental issues.

Compensation to Victims (4Principle 22)

The States should join to further the scope of international law for prescribing liability for those harming the environment. States should also come together to compensate victims of environmental pollution or damage.

Cooperation (Principles 24 and 25)

Principle 24: Cooperation with nations – Although each state has exclusive jurisdiction to legislate on internal matters, international cooperation is necessary for the holistic improvement of the environment. States must recognize that environmental problems affect all the states equally. By multilateral and bilateral agreements states can control, prevent, and reduce environmental risks.

Principle 25: Coordination with nations – Coordination between states is crucial for alleviating the existing conditions. The states can jointly coordinate actions and plans for improving existing environmental conditions.

Other principles

Principle 11: Environmental Policy – The environmental policy of every nation should be progressive. The policies of every state must enhance and complement each other. The policies shouldn't restrict or adversely affect developing countries. National and international organizations should strive for better living conditions for all without affecting the environment.

Principle 19: Education in environmental matters – Education is one of the tools to spread awareness about the pathetic state of the environment. The underprivileged, poor, illiterate should have access to education. Education broadens the mind. Awareness about the existing conditions is necessary so that people can jointly tackle environmental matters.

Principle 20: Expanding scientific research – Researching and developing methods nationally and internationally is important to tackle environmental problems. There must exist a system where information and research can flow easily across nations. Countries must also control their spending on scientific research without burdening the economy.

Principle 9: Environmental Deficiencies – Natural disasters and underdevelopment lead to deficiencies. Navigating through such deficiencies is difficult. Requesting technological and financial assistance to supplement the local efforts leads to a quicker and effective remedy.

Principle 10: Stability of prices and incomes – Stability in the prices of essential commodities and stability of income is essential for the environmental management of developing countries. Economic factors are also part of the environmental process.

Principle 12: Education on environmental protection – Environmental protection is the need of the hour. Every citizen should understand the importance of environmental protection. Adoption of a suitable medium like social media, print media, etc. is crucial to spread awareness about environmental protection.

Principle 16: Population Control – In areas where the population is excessive and is likely to affect the environment, the states can implement policies to control the growth of the population. These policies shouldn't violate basic human rights. In today's world overpopulation is one of the major reasons for the depletion of natural resources.

Principle 17: Setting up of national institutions – States should establish national bodies for the control and management of environmental resources within the state.

Principle 23: Implementing a national agenda – The states may find that certain procedures and rules may not align the value system of the country. In that case, the states need not follow such a procedure. The states are also exempted if such procedures cause unwarranted social costs.

Principle 26: Ban on nuclear weapons – Nuclear weapons is the most destructive weapons. They cause more damage to the environment than any other weapon. All the nations should come together to ban nuclear weapons.

III. Effects of the Convention

The Stockholm convention paved the way for other international conventions on the preservation of the environment such as the Convention on International Trade on Endangered Species of Wild Flora and Fauna, 1973.[35] In the same line, the Parliament of India passed the Air (Prevention and Control of Pollution) Act, 1981,[36] the Water (Prevention and Control of Pollution) Act, 1974,[37] and the Forest Conservation Act, 1980[38] to give effect to the Stockholm convention.

The Stockholm convention was the first convention to discuss environmental issues on a global scale. The declaration proclaims truths relating to man and the environment such as man is the creator and moulders of his surroundings. The declaration also reiterates the importance of preservation of the environment. It urges citizens to come together and protect the environment. The declaration recognizes humans as the greatest threat to the environment. Humans are responsible for almost all of the environmental destruction. Humans have altered the human environment also.

---

35. *Convention on International Trade in Endangered Species of Wild Fauna and Flora.*
36. The Air (Prevention and Control of Pollution) Act, 1981, No. 14 of 1981. (1981). Ministry of Environment, Forest and Climate Change, Government of India.
37. The Water (Prevention and Control of Pollution) Act, 1974, No. 6 of 1974. (1974). Ministry of Environment, Forest and Climate Change, Government of India.
38. The Forest (Conservation) Act, 1980, No. 69 of 1980. (1980). Ministry of Environment, Forest and Climate Change, Government of India.

The declaration discusses in detail the role of underdeveloped nations in environmental problems and urges them to reduce their negative impact on the environment. The industrial countries are not free from problems, but their problems relate to industrialization and technological development.

The significance of humans and their contributions to the environment are also discussed in detail. The declaration recognizes the capability of humans to make strides in social progress and the use of science to make a better environment. Individuals have the responsibility to exercise care and precaution. Ignorant and careless actions lead to the destruction and deterioration of the environment. To take careful action, better awareness, and education about the protection of the environment are required.

Governments are directed to control their internal actions by enacting and enforcing environmental laws and to coordinate with other nations and international agencies to mitigate the damage caused by pollution.

IV. Problems and Challenges

The declaration contains sound principles and beautiful proclamations, however, the wordings of the declaration are unclear and ambiguous at certain points. Almost 48 years since adopting the declaration the condition of the environment has worsened.

The presence of CO_2 (Carbon Dioxide) has increased by 26 percent since 1970. This results in greater global warming which has detrimental effects all around the globe. More than 700,000 sq.km of the Amazon rainforest were cleared for farming since the '70s. The condition of other forested areas is not much better.

Some estimates paint a darker picture, such as the number of fishes in the oceans has almost dropped by 50 %. The quality of the oceans is also not that great. These numbers and reports reveal the gap between planning and taking action. The way ahead is also not easy. Taking action is the only way to tackle environmental depletion. The laws should adopt more stringent actions. No amount of conventions will help in environmental development unless people start taking action. We should realize the current situation and act cautiously.

V. Stockholm Conference, 1972 and India

In 1972 in Stockholm, Sweden, the United Nations facilitated its first Conference on the Human Environment, the official statement of which is ordinarily called the Stockholm Declaration of 1972. The 26 standards inside the assertion comprehensively perceive human effect on the earth, implying without precedent for history that ecological issues have been tended to openly and on a worldwide scale. The affirmation underscores the requirement for countries to structure integrative advancement designs that join science and innovation so as to decrease air, land, and water contamination and human effect on nature.[39] It asks every country to make guidelines for ensuring untamed life and moderating the normal assets that are accessible inside that nation, and recommends making national populace approaches, since overpopulation intensifies the strain on characteristic assets.

The Stockholm Declaration gave an establishment to a significant number of the ecological arrangements that have been set up in the 113 taking interest nations. Moreover, the center standards introduced in the statement and the conversations that prompted it started the making of the United Nations Environmental Program, which has accordingly grown progressively explicit conventions to ensure the earth.

VI. Stockholm Principle Regarding Wildlife Conservation

"Man has a special responsibility to safeguard and wisely manage the heritage of wildlife and its habitat which are now gravely imperiled by a combination of adverse factors. Nature conservation including wildlife must therefore receive importance in planning for economic development".

This conference also had a great impact on the environmental related laws. After the year 1972, India enacted the Water Act of 1976, Environment Protection Act of 1986, Air Act of 1981 and many other policies and notifications of environmental law.

------

39. United Nations. (1972). *Stockholm Declaration on the Human Environment*. United Nations Conference on the Human Environment

Objective

As given in Article 1, the objective of the Stockholm Convention is to protect human health and the environment (forest, wildlife, etc.) from persistent organic pollutants.

Result of the Convention -Wildlife Protection Act, 1972

The act provides the safety and promises to protect the country's wild animals, birds, flora and faunas, and plant species with the aim of ensuring environmental and ecological balance and security. The act also lays down the punishments on hunting various animal species. The act was last amended in year 2006. An amendment bill was introduced in Rajya Sabha in the year 2013 naming it a Standing committee, but later in year 2015, it was withdrawn.[40]

The Government enacted this act with the initial motive of effectively protecting the wildlife of the country and to control poaching, illegal trading and smuggling in wildlife and its derivatives. After the amendment of 2003, the punishments and penalties of the crimes and offenses related were made more strict and stringent. The government has proposed and is continuously working to provide more amendments in the law and to strengthen this act it will introduce more rigid measures in this act as to provide protection to he listed endangered wildlife animals, plants, flora and fauna and other important parts of our ecosystem.

---

40. Wildlife Protection Act, 1972, No. 53 of 1972. (1972). Ministry of Environment, Forest and Climate Change, Government of India. Last amended 2006. An amendment bill was introduced in the Rajya Sabha in 2013 but was withdrawn in 2015.

Chapter 4

The Constitutionality of The Wildlife Act

- **ARTICLE 48A**[41]- of the Constitution of India directs the State to improve and protect the environment and the safeguard wildlife and forests. This article was added in the 42nd Amendment in year 1976.

- **ARTICLE 51A(g)**-[42]of the Constitution imposes certain fundamental duties for the People in India and one of them is to protect and improve natural environment that includes lakes, forests, rivers and wildlife and to have compassion for living creatures of the environment.

I. Historical Background

- The First law related to it was passed officially by the British Government in the year 1887 and was known to be the Wild Birds Protection Act, 1887. The law made the possession and sale of wild birds which were either killed or were captured illegally[43].

- During the British Era, Wildlife Protection was not given a priority; it was just then in 1960 that the issues of the protection of Wildlife and the prevention of Endangered species from becoming extinct came into the force.

- In the year 1912, a second law was enacted which was famously known as the Wildlife Birds and Animals Protection Act. This was further amended

---

41. The Constitution of India, 1950, Article 48-A
42. The Constitution of India, 1950, Article 51A(g)
43. Government of India. (1887). The Wild Birds Protection Act, 1887

in 1935 when the Wildlife Birds and Animals Protection (Amendment) Act, 1935 was passed.[44]

II. Need for the Wildlife Conservation and Wildlife Protection Act, 1972

Wildlife is an important part of our nature which cannot be left out, and so it was included as the state subject until the parliament passed their laws in the year 1972.[45]

The need to make a nationwide law in the domain of environment especially for wildlife includes the following:

1. India is a hub filled with varied flora and fauna. Various species during the 90's period were seen declining rapidly in numbers, for example: during 20th century, India was very close to 40000 tigers but by the seventies, there was drastic reduction in number up to 1820.

2. There was a drastic imbalance in the number of flora and fauna which caused ecological degradation and effected climate and the ecosystem in those times and now too.

3. The numbers of national parks in India prior to this enactment of Wildlife protection act were only five.

4. There was most recent act which was passed during British times of Wild Birds and Animals Protection, 1935 which needed to be upgraded regarding the punishments awarded to the poachers and illegal wildlife traders.

a) **Salient features and initiatives taken by the government for wildlife conservation**

In Wildlife Protection act, 1972 there were many essential features and important rules put up by the government for the welfare of wildlife sectors in the act which is as under:

---

44. The Wildlife Birds and Animals Protection (Amendment) Act, 1935

45. The Wildlife Protection Act, 1972

1. The act prohibits killing and hunting of Endangered species.

2. The act provides the advisory boards for the formation of advisory boards for wildlife conservation, wildlife wardens, specify their powers and their duties.

3. It was for the first time that a comprehensive list of the endangered wildlife species of the country was prepared.

4. It helped India become a party to the Convention on International Trade in Endangered Species of Flora and Fauna (CITES), where CITES became a multinational treaty with the endangered animals and plants.

5. The act provided for the establishment of wildlife sanctuaries, national parks, etc.

6. The act also provided for the establishment of National tiger Conservation Authority, which is a statutory body of the Ministry Of Environment, Forest and Climate Change.

7. The act maintains the strength and gives rise and power to Tiger Conservation In India.

8. The act introduced Six Schedules which gave varying degrees of protection to classes of Flora and Fauna in which:

•   Schedule 1 and Schedule 2 (part II) includes absolute protection and offences under these schedules which also brings us with maximum penalties.

•   Schedules also include species which may be hunted down.

b)   Importance of wildlife for the development of human and the society

Untamed life has assumed a significant job in the advancement of dress, clinical materials, trial models, and logical exploration. Creature skins and hide have been utilized for attire for centuries, and even today are images of style. Wild creatures have likewise given sustenance to people, framing a critical extent of our eating routine. At the beginning phase of Homo sapiens, wide-spread cultivating and fundamental arrangement of farming creation expanded human food bounty and assortment, which again added to an expansion in mind volume. At the late phase of Homo sapiens, with the appearance of essential horticulture, creature cultivation, and the modern insurgency, the structure, propensity, and idea of the human eating routine has tended towards dependability. Correspondingly, the physical structure has remained prevalently unaltered Clinical progression has additionally been critical in the advancement of people. Untamed life additionally gives crude materials to logical and clinical exploration.

People and natural life are firmly interrelated, particularly with respect to culture, customary drugs, food, chasing, and eco-the travel industry. Subsequently, it is difficult and suitable to isolate natural life from human. It is both socially and logically significant, in this manner, that we explain how best to ensure natural life and whereupon idea of untamed life preservation this insurance is based.

The world isn't ecologically uniform. Countries vary in their natural assets, in terms of value and amount. Taking into consideration, there are no single arrangement works wherever to ensure environment protection. The ecological imbalances on the planet are resembled by financial ones, which are significant deterrents to fulfill the fundamental human needs, particularly in creating nations, and an obstruction to the amicable advancement of humankind. The monetary advancement currently appreciated by the created nations was in some cases accomplished without due respect to the safeguarding of human condition, and today they are considered as the bosses of human rights defenders. In any case, it is properly brought up that the overall standards and solutions of universal law are appropriate to the issues of transnational contamination and ecological debasement. Along these lines, the worldwide condition has been satisfactorily ensured through Local, Regional, National and International laws, Policies, Treaties and Conventions and they maintained the balance in the ecology especially in the country like India.

Today when people are concern about corruption in wildlife sectors, degradation of the nature throughout the world, and sad results of this, customary morals of environment conservation and protection could be seen as a source of inspiration and direction to the future generations. Maybe no other culture can give such a significant assortment of social practices and naturally stabled relationship with nature as the Indian culture. Wildlife sector obviously needs new strategies developments and strictness regarding its punishments of illegal wildlife trading and crimes increasing day by day.

c) Recommendations

- More explores ought to be accomplished for featuring the current issues about wildlife, environment issues, biodiversity and endeavor has been accomplished for protection of biodiversity.

- There is a solid need to joint effort of Government furthermore, Stakeholders with NGOs for various projects worry to protection of biodiversity and natural life government assistance.

- Government ought to endorse enactment for illicit exercises that drives biodiversity to the edge of termination.

- There ought to be open mindfulness about wildlife conservation significance through social, print and electronic media.

- Students study visit ought to be orchestrated at school, school what's more, college level for giving mindfulness about the significance of biodiversity and essential activities for its preservation.

Chapter 5
Agenda 21

Agenda 21 is a comprehensive plan of action to be taken globally, nationally and locally by organizations of the United Nations System, Governments, and Major Groups in every area in which human impacts on the environment Agenda 21, the Rio Declaration on Environment and Development, and the Statement of principles for the Sustainable Management of Forests were adopted by more than 178 Governments at the United Nations Conference on Environment and Development (UNCED) held in Rio de Janeiro, Brazil, 3 to 14 June 1992.[46]

The Commission on Sustainable Development (CSD) was created in December 1992 to ensure effective follow-up of UNCED, to monitor and report on implementation of the agreements at the local, national, regional and international levels. It was agreed that a five year review of Earth Summit progress would be made in 1997 by the United Nations General Assembly meeting in special session.

The full implementation of Agenda 21, the Programme for Further Implementation of Agenda 21 and the Commitments to the Rio principles, were strongly reaffirmed at the World Summit on Sustainable Development (WSSD) held in Johannesburg, South Africa from 26 August to 4 September 2002. It came into existence at the Rio Earth Summit in the year 1992 and the slogan for Agenda 21 was **"think globally and act locally"**.

---

46. United Nations. (1992). *Agenda 21: Programme of action for sustainable development.* United Nations Conference on Environment and Development (UNCED), Rio de Janeiro, Brazil, 3-14 June 1992

I. The Objectives of Agenda 21 are as Follows

1. It aims for achieving Global Sustainable Development.

2. It is an agenda to fight environmental damage, poverty, disease etc.

3. In agenda 21, needs of shared responsibilities were discussed. example: polio drops.

4. One of its major objectives is that every local govt. should draw its own agenda 21.

Chapter 6
Environmental Crime

I. Environmental Crime in India

Environmental crime is a term describing illegal activities that convey abusive harm to the natural environment, such as illegal logging, pollution, and unregulated extraction of resources. Most of the time, they affect Indigenous peoples more seriously due to their lifestyle, culture, and livelihoods closely connected to their natural surroundings. This abstract presents the interplay of environmental crime and Indigenous peoples, in particular, how such environmental degradation affects the rights and well-being of Indigenous peoples through illegal activities.

For generations, indigenous communities have proved the fact that they can coexist with their environments by engaging in sustainable practices and applying traditional knowledge. However, with the incursion of industrial activities and exploitation of natural resources, some environmental crimes such as deforestation, pollution, land grabbing, among others, have increased tremendously. These activities are not only going to upset the ecological balance but also violate the rights of Indigenous people over their land and resources.

Case studies from the Amazon rainforest and the Indian subcontinent demonstrate how environmental crimes have directly impacted Indigenous communities. Illegal mining and deforestation in the Amazon pose a threat to both health and culture for the Yanomami tribe. Mining operations in India not only ignore the land rights of Indigenous communities but also their traditional practices of environmental conversation.

International treaties and national laws designed to protect indigenous rights and the environment are typically very weakly equipped against these issues. Infringement issues, such as corruption and poor legal recognition of land rights, still exacerbate the problem.

This abstract serves to advance a more resolute and holistic approach with respect to the rights of Indigenous peoples for environmental protection. Strengthening legal protections, enhancing community involvement in governance, and promoting sustainable development are imperatives to reduce the impacts of environmental crimes and to achieve justice for Indigenous communities.

Environmental crime encompasses all activities that relate to the environment and are illegal, such as illegal logging, wildlife trafficking, pollution, and resource extraction. It tends to heavily impact Indigenous communities whose livelihoods, culture, and spirituality have been entrenched in the environment. Indigenous people, who have always been custodians of their lands, are usually the first ones to bear the brunt of environmental crimes.[47]

Indigenous communities have unique knowledge systems—what is termed Traditional Ecological Knowledge, developed over centuries. It forms the basis for sustainable management of natural resources. Despite that fact, Indigenous Peoples are oftentimes marginalized, discriminated against, and even murdered for protecting their lands and the environment against illegal activities.[48] This article examines the connection between environmental crime and Indigenous peoples: their historical context, the forms of environmental crime affecting them, and the legal protection frameworks of their rights[49].

II. History of the Environment in India

India is a land of divergent ecosystems—from the mighty Himalayas to the vast Thar Desert. The Indian subcontinent has its share of rich environmental history that has been shaped by natural processes, human activity, and socio-

---

47. J. O'Brien and Y. Lin, The United States National Park System: Overview, Challenges and Policy Recommendations for China, 3 J. Envtl. L. and Pol'y 106, 106-57 (2023)

48. K. Göcke, *Indigenous Peoples in International Law* (2017),

49. Smith, J. (2020). *Indigenous Rights and Environmental Justice*. Green Earth Press

political factors over millennia[50]. The interaction of man and the environment is embedded within its culture, religion, and economic traditions in the case of India. To appreciate the environmental problems facing the world today, one needs to understand the history behind all this, which went on to appreciate the legal regimes developed to address these problems[51].

A) Ancient and medieval periods

The environmental history of India goes back to ancient times, when the world was natural and reverent, protected as part of religious and cultural practices. This is reflected in the Vedic texts, ranging in date from about 1500 BCE to 500 BCE, where there is an emphasis laid on the elements of nature: air, water, earth, and forests. One of the oldest known texts, Rigveda, includes hymns that not only express respect but celebrate the very forces of Nature.[52]

During the Mauryan Empire, Emperor Ashoka, influenced by his embracing of Buddhism, encouraged the planting of trees and the setting up of wildlife reserves and irrigation facilities in the period (322-185 BCE). His rock edicts show concern for the well-being of all living beings, animals and plants alike, and could very well be considered one of the earlier types of environmental governance.

This medieval period, especially the empire of the Mughals (1526-1857), laid out extensive gardens and so promoted agriculture and forest conservation for the sport of hunting. While indulging in the bounties of nature, the Mughals appreciated the principles of managing it sustainably. Shikar or royal hunting was not merely a sport but a control over the population of animals for maintaining the ecological balance.

---

50. T. Pullaiah and K.J. Reddy, *Biodiversity in India* (Daya Books 2002).
51. P. Claeys and M. Edelman, The United Nations Declaration on the Rights of Peasants and Other People Working in Rural Areas, 47 J. PEASANT STUD. 1 (2019)
52. Oldenberg H, *The Religion of the Veda* (Motilal Banarsidass 1988)

B) Colonial period

Of course, the arrival of the British in the 17th century was a turning point for India's environmental history. The British colonial administration did not hesitate to treat the natural resources of India as something that could be freely used for profit-making purposes[53]. The huge demand generated in the country due to railway expansion and agriculture resulted in large areas of India's forests being cleared by the timber industry during this period. The colonial forest policies, especially the Indian Forest Act of 1865 and its later amendment in 1878[54], were actually designed for controlling and commercializing forests at the cost of the local communities who had lived in harmony with such ecosystems for hundreds of years.[55]

The colonial government introduced land revenue systems, of which the Permanent Settlement of Bengal in 1793 changed age-long traditional land use practices and caused agricultural land degradation. Emphasis on cash crops like indigo, cotton, and opium cropped up with the depletion of soil fertility and the decline of traditional subsistence farming.[56]

The colonial government introduced land revenue systems like Permanent Settlement. British environmental management was oriented toward utilitarian extraction rather than resource conservation. It had long-lasting effects on India's environment by destroying forests, wildlife habitats, and disrupting the traditional methods of agriculture.

C) Post-independence period

It also initiated land revenue systems like the Permanent Settlement by the colonial government. The British had adopted a utilitarian approach to environmental management, extracting. After the independence of India in

---

53. Jones, A. (2015). *Colonialism and Environmental Change in India*. Historical Press.

54. Government of India. (1865). Indian Forest Act, 1865. No. 16 of 1865. Ministry of Environment, Forest and Climate Change, Government of India. Last amended 1878

55. Government of India. (1865). Indian Forest Act, 1865. No. 16 of 1865. Ministry of Environment, Forest and Climate Change, Government of India. Last amended 187

56. Manjapra K, *Colonialism in Global Perspective* (Cambridge University Press 2020)

1947, the newly formed government was left with the task of rebuilding the nation's economy while arresting the environmental degradation inherited from the colonial rulers. During the early years, attention was directed toward industrialization and agricultural expansion at most times at the cost of environmental sustainability. The Green Revolution in the 1960s achieved certain gains in food production but at the cost of overexploitation of chemical fertilizers, pesticides, and water resources, which degraded the soil, polluted water, and led to biodiversity loss.[57]

However, with the post-independence period, environmental consciousness started to take roots and enactment of legal framework was being developed in order to protect the environment. Such important legislation enacted in order to protect India's natural resources includes the Wildlife Protection Act of 1972, the Forest Conservation Act of 1980, and the Environment (Protection) Act of 1986.[58]

The Chipko Movement of the 1970s is probably one of the most symbolic grassroots environmental movements in India, in which rural women from the Himalayan region embraced trees to prevent their felling. The movement was a classic case of community participation in the conservation process and has since gone on to raise public awareness of the need for forest and biodiversity conservation.[59]

III. Historical Context

The indigenous people have lived in harmony with nature for thousands of years since they have the availability of deep insight into the ecosystems, which allowed them to support their communities. The practices of agriculture, hunting, and water management, inherent in their traditional knowledge, were important to the preservation of biodiversity and the ecological balance.

---

57. R Black and others, *'Environment of Peace: Security in a New Era of Risk'* (2022)
58. Wildlife Protection Act, 1972
59. S Jewitt, *Environment, Knowledge and Gender: Local Development in India's Jharkhand* (Routledge 2019)

Then, colonial powers arrived and disrupted these practices through the dispossession of Indigenous lands and erosion of their cultural heritage.

Alien legal regimes often ignored indigenous land tenure systems, or at worst introduced land grabbing and environmental degradation. Extractive industries, such as mining and logging, joined the fray in inflicting environmental damage and destabilizing the very bases of indigenous livelihoods[60]. It was through institutionalization in laws and policies that Indigenous communities were made subaltern, always serving colonial powers' and later postcolonial states' interests.

The colonialism legacy survives to date in the non-inclusion of indigenous peoples in decision-making over lands and resources affecting them. Environmental crimes are frequent occurrences in areas remote and richly resourced, with adverse impacts on indigenous communities, ranging from loss of lands, livelihoods, and cultural identity

IV. Types of Environmental Crimes Affecting Indigenous People

Environmental crimes take various forms, each with devastating consequences for Indigenous communities. These crimes often intersect with other human rights violations, such as forced displacement, violence, and the destruction of cultural heritage.

A) Deforestation and illegal logging

The most far-reaching environmental crimes against indigenous people occur through deforestation, with special focus on the tropical areas like the Amazon rainforest. Illegal logging, mainly due to the increasing demand for timber and expansion of agricultural land, clears huge areas of forests and threatens the very existence of indigenous communities. Forest loss takes from the indigenous people more than a place to live and their sources of food but also

---

60. IC Carney and others, *'Gender-Based Violence and Environment Linkages: The Violence of Inequality'* (2020)

unsettles the precarious balance of ecosystems on which they depend for their cultural and spiritual practices.[61]

Most of the time, illegal logging is carried out by large criminal syndicates that act with the impunity so often involving connivance with local authorities. Indigenous leaders who stand in the way of such operations face intimidation, violence, and even assassination[62]. It also contributes to climate change, thereby exacerbating the vulnerabilities of indigenous communities who are already at the forefront of environmental degradation.

B) Mining and resource extraction

Mining and extraction, particularly in countries with high mineral, oil, and gas content, are among the main contributing factors to environmental crimes. Lands of indigenous peoples are generally the target of these operations, as multinational corporations and state-owned enterprises believe that these areas are covered with valuable resources. This has resulted in dangerous environmental deterioration, manifested in polluted water, contaminated soil, and clear-cutting.

Indigenous communities are very often in opposition to mining and resource extraction projects on their lands; indeed, the activities are threatening not only their environment but also their rights to self-determination and cultural preservation. Their resistance is very often met with violence, criminalization, and forced displacement. This is further worsened by the lack of legal recognition of indigenous peoples' land rights, wherein most of these indigenous communities do not have formal titles over their ancestral lands, which are often easily exploited by corporations.[63]

61. Katila P, et al, *Sustainable Development Goals* (Cambridge University Press 2019)

62. Acebes CM and Wilkinson D, *Rainforest Mafias: How Violence and Impunity Fuel Deforestation in Brazil's Amazon* (Zed Books 2019)

63. Postero N, *The Indigenous State: Race, Politics, and Performance in Plurinational Bolivia* (2017)

C) Pollution and contamination of water sources

It is a common environmental crime across the country that indigenous peoples bear a disproportionate burden of pollution and contamination of water sources. Some examples of industrial activities that end up contaminating rivers, lakes, and groundwater—major sources of water crucial to the survival of Indigenous communities—are mining, oil drilling, and agricultural runoff. Contaminating water sources can lead to a variety of health issues: from waterborne diseases to reproductive health problems and the loss of traditional food sources.

Many times, communities are not informed of potential environmental hazards from industrial activities on their lands. Lack of access to clean water is a violation of their basic human rights and undermines their capacity to maintain their traditional ways of life. Contaminating water sources has spiritual implications for indigenous people as well because water is considered a sacrament by them and forms the core of their cultural and religious practices.[64]

D) Land grabbing and forced evictions

Corporations and state authorities have recourse to land grabbing and forced evictions as a way to access indigenous lands for industrial activities. Very often, these are conducted without the free, prior, and informed consent of Indigenous communities, which are in violation of international human rights standards. Land grabbing does not only deprive Indigenous peoples of their homes and livelihoods but also leads to the destruction of their cultural heritage, therefore causing the loss of identity.

Evictions are often carried out with violence, harassment, and property destruction, thereby leaving indigenous communities vulnerable and displaced. The lack of legal recognition of indigenous land rights makes it very hard to redress or hold the perpetrators accountable. Many a time, indigenous people are forcefully relocated to cities or resettlement camps where they continue to be marginalized further into poverty.

---

64. Grant P, *State of the World's Minorities and Indigenous Peoples 2016: Focus on Culture and Heritage* (Minority Rights Group 2016)

V. Case Studies

To illustrate the impact of environmental crimes on Indigenous people, this section examines three case studies from different parts of the world.

A) THE AMAZON RAINFOREST AND THE YANOMAMI TRIBE

The Amazon rainforest is home to a diverse range of Indigenous communities, including the Yanomami tribe, who have lived in the region for thousands of years. The Yanomami have a deep spiritual connection to the forest, which they consider sacred and essential for their survival. However, their way of life is under threat from illegal mining activities, particularly gold mining, which has led to the destruction of large areas of forest and the contamination of rivers with mercury.[65]

The presence of illegal miners, known as garimpeiros, has brought violence, disease, and environmental destruction to the Yanomami territory. The mercury used in gold mining has contaminated the rivers, leading to severe health problems for the Yanomami, including neurological disorders and birth defects. The Brazilian government has been criticized for its failure to protect the Yanomami and their lands, despite international pressure and legal obligations.

B) STERLITE COPPER PLANT CASE (THOOTHUKUDI, TAMIL NADU)

Background: Sterlite, the subsidiary of Vedanta Ltd., had a copper smelter at Thoothukudi, Tamil Nadu that was in operation for over two decades. This plant faced several accusations of flouting environmental violations, related to air and water pollution, affecting health and the livelihood of local communities, including indigenous fishing communities[66].

---

65. F-ML Tourneau, 'The Sustainability Challenges of Indigenous Territories in Brazil's Amazonia' (2015) 14 *Current Opinion in Environmental Sustainability* 213

66. *State of Tamil Nadu v Sterlite Industries (India) Ltd* (Civil Appeal No 4347 of 2019, Supreme Court of India).

Legal Issues: The case involved violations of the Environmental Protection Act, 1986, and the Water (Prevention and Control of Pollution) Act, 1974. Further, the company's activity infringed on the Right to Life under Article 21 of the Constitution, as the pollution was very hazardous to health for the indigenous people.

Judgment: The TNPCB ordered closure of the plant in 2018 after years of sustained protests and protracted litigation. Thereafter, by its order, the NGT permitted the Sterlite plant to reopen but this order was stayed by the Supreme Court thereby effectively upholding the closure imposed by the TNPCB.

Influence: This case reiterated that the legal principle has to be basically based on a rational balance between protection of the environment and the need for economic development; however, corporate entities cannot violate environmental laws at the cost of indigenous people's rights.

C) THE STANDING ROCK SIOUX TRIBE AND THE DAKOTA ACCESS PIPELINE

The Standing Rock Sioux Tribe in the USA made global headlines in 2016 through their opposition to the proposed construction of the Dakota Access Pipeline. The pipeline was intended to transport crude oil from North Dakota to Illinois across the Missouri River, which is the main source of drinking water for the Standing Rock Sioux. The concerns of the tribe over this pipeline were visibly based on potential oil spills that might ruin their supply of water and culturally very significantly affect them.[67]

The resistance of the tribe to this pipeline bilingualized into a massive movement, where thousands of indigenous and nonindigenous people camped out in protests at Standing Rock. Heavily armed law enforcement responded with tear gas, water cannons, and rubber bullets. The pipeline was finished in 2017 despite the efforts of the tribe, although the system's operation remains bogged down in the courts.

---

67. MacCarald C, *The Standing Rock Sioux Challenge the Dakota Access Pipeline* (North Star Editions, Inc 2019)

D) INDIGENOUS COMMUNITIES IN INDIA AND THEIR STRUGGLES AGAINST MINING CORPORATIONS

India has a very large population of indigenous people often called Scheduled Tribes who are located in resource-rich areas. Over time, these areas, rich in minerals and many other valuable resources have become hotbeds of conflict as mining corporations come in to extract them. In many cases, mining activities associated with the forced displacement of the indigenous people and environmental destruction are considered to be an infringement of the basic rights of these very people whose benefits and compensation are very inadequate. The book also exercises a legal analysis of the struggles that these communities are waging against mining corporations through Indian laws and international legal regimes.

Legal Regime Governing the Rights of the Indigenous Peoples: There are a number of safeguards enshrined in the Indian Constitution for the indigenous people, keeping in view their identity as a group of people separated from the mainstream and requiring special protection. Article 244 of the Constitution empowers the state to frame special laws for Scheduled Areas and Scheduled Tribes. The Fourth Schedule identifies the states and territories of India, designating majorly as scheduled areas, where the Fifth and Sixth Schedules of the Indian Constitution provide for administrative and control jurisdictions over these scheduled areas with a view to protecting indigenous peoples from exploitation.

The next major legislation, therefore, includes the Panchayats Extension to Scheduled Areas Act, 1996 (PESA)[68], and the Forest Rights Act, 2006 (FRA)[69], both of which recognize indigenous people's rights over land and resources. Under PESA, it has been provided that the Gram Sabhas of every village in Scheduled Areas shall be empowered to manage natural resources, and lastly, it gives them a major say in matters pertaining to their land. The FRA goes further to bolster such rights by recognizing the traditional forest

---

68. The Panchayats Extension to Scheduled Areas Act, 1996. Ministry of Panchayati Raj
69. The Scheduled Tribes and Other Traditional Forest Dwellers (Recognition of Forest Rights) Act, 2006. Ministry of Tribal Affair

rights of the indigenous communities in regard to the ownership, access, and even use of forest resources.

Judicial Precedents and Indigenous Struggles: Indian judiciary has played a very important role in dealing with the agitating indigenous communities whose lives have been disturbed by activities of mining. In response to the cases filed, some landmark judgments have been passed to uphold the cause of indigenous rights and environmental justice. In the judgment of Samatha v. State of Andhra Pradesh (1997)[70], the Supreme Court ruled that land of the government in Scheduled Areas could not be transferred to non-tribal entities, including mining corporations, without the consent of the Gram Sabha. This was a very major victory for indigenous communities in the sense that it had effectively strengthened constitutional and statutory protections available for them.

Another important case is that of Niyamgiri Suraksha Samiti v. Union of India[71], in which the Supreme Court upheld the rights of Dongria Kondh people over the Niyamgiri Hills in Odisha, stating that prior consent from Gram Sabha is necessary before zeroing in on any mining operation in the area. This decision set up the right to community involvement in decisions by institutions affecting their lands and resources.[72].

VI. Legal Framework and Protection

A) International legal instruments

The international legal frameworks play a great role in protecting indigenous rights from environmental crimes. Two very essential instruments that can confirm the rights of indigenous people over their lands, territories, and resources are: the United Nations Declaration on the Rights of Indigenous Peoples and the International Labour Organization's Convention 169.

---

70. Samatha v. State of Andhra Pradesh, (1997) 8 SCC 191 (India)

71. [2017] AIR SC 245

72. *State of the World's Minorities and Indigenous Peoples 2016: Focus on Culture and Heritage* (Minority Rights Group 2016)

UNDRIP underlines that without free, prior, and informed consent, nothing can be done in the domain of development projects on Indigenous lands. ILO Convention 169 concerns the standard-setting that should prevail for the protection of indigenous peoples and participation of indigenous peoples in decision-making processes.[73]

B) National laws and policies

At the national level, many countries have enacted laws and policies aimed at safeguarding Indigenous rights. These include constitutional provisions, land rights legislation, and environmental protection laws. However, the effectiveness of these laws varies widely, with some countries providing strong protections and others lacking comprehensive frameworks. National laws often intersect with international obligations, creating a complex legal landscape for protecting Indigenous communities.

C) Indian Laws Protecting Environmental Law

The rich natural heritage and diversified ecosystems of India necessitate a stringent legal framework to protect and conserve the environment effectively. Over the decades, India has built up an enormous body of environmental laws related to protecting the environment, conservation efforts, and sustainable development. These laws demonstrate India's commitment to upholding environmental rights as enshrined in the Constitution and fulfilling the obligations arising under international environmental agreements. The major Indian legislations in force to protect environmental law, the extent and efficacy of those laws, and problems associated with their implementation will be discussed in the present paper.

---

73. Cittadino F, *Incorporating Indigenous Rights in the International Regime on Biodiversity Protection: Access, Benefit-Sharing and Conservation in Indigenous Lands* (BRILL 2019)

VII. Constitutional Provisions

The Constitution of India, which came into force in 1950, contains several provisions that directly and indirectly protect the environment. Two key articles underscore the importance of environmental protection:

- **Article 48A**[74]: Introduced by the 42nd Amendment in 1976, Article 48A places a duty on the State to protect and improve the environment and to safeguard the forests and wildlife of the country. This Directive Principle of State Policy, though non-justiciable, sets the tone for environmental governance in India.

- **Article 51A (g)**[75]: Also added by the 42nd Amendment, Article 51A (g) imposes a fundamental duty on every citizen to protect and improve the natural environment, including forests, lakes, rivers, and wildlife, and to have compassion for living creatures.

These constitutional provisions form the bedrock of India's environmental legal framework, guiding both legislative action and judicial interpretation.

VIII. Key Environmental Laws in India

India's environmental laws are a mix of comprehensive statutes, sector-specific regulations, and judicial pronouncements. Some of the most significant environmental laws include:

A) The Environment (Protection) Act, 1986

The Environment (Protection) Act, 1986[76], is the cornerstone of India's environmental legislation. Enacted in the wake of the Bhopal gas tragedy, this Act provides a framework for the protection and improvement of the environment. The Act grants the central government wide-ranging powers to regulate all activities that have the potential to harm the environment. It empowers the government to establish standards for emissions and effluents,

---

74. Constitution of India 1950, art 48A
75. Constitution of India 1950, art 51A(g)
76. Environment (Protection) Act 1986

regulate hazardous substances, and take necessary measures to prevent environmental pollution.

B) The Water (Prevention and Control of Pollution) Act, 1974

The Water (Prevention and Control of Pollution) Act, 1974[77], is one of the earliest environmental laws in India, aimed at preventing and controlling water pollution. The Act establishes Central and State Pollution Control Boards, which are responsible for monitoring water quality and enforcing pollution control measures. The Act also prescribes penalties for non-compliance with pollution control standards, making it a critical tool in protecting India's water resources.

C) The Air (Prevention and Control of Pollution) Act, 1981

Similar to the Water Act, the Air (Prevention and Control of Pollution) Act, 1981[78], focuses on preventing and controlling air pollution. It empowers the Central and State Pollution Control Boards to set air quality standards, regulate emissions from industrial and vehicular sources, and take measures to reduce air pollution. The Act also provides for penalties and punishments for violations of air quality standards.

D) The Wildlife (Protection) Act, 1972

The Wildlife (Protection) Act, 1972[79], is a comprehensive law aimed at protecting India's wildlife and biodiversity. The Act establishes protected areas such as national parks, wildlife sanctuaries, and conservation reserves, and provides for the regulation of hunting, poaching, and trade in wildlife. It also sets up various authorities, including the National and State Boards for Wildlife, to oversee wildlife conservation efforts

---

77. The Water (Prevention and Control of Pollution) Act, 1974
78. The Air (Prevention and Control of Pollution) Act, 1981
79. The Wildlife (Protection) Act, 1972

E) The Forest (Conservation) Act, 1980

The Forest (Conservation) Act, 1980[80], seeks to regulate the diversion of forest land for non-forest purposes, such as industrial and infrastructure development. The Act requires prior approval from the central government for any such diversion, ensuring that forest conservation is given due consideration in development projects. The Act also provides for the imposition of conditions, including compensatory afforestation, to mitigate the environmental impact of forest land diversion.

F) The National Green Tribunal Act, 2010

The National Green Tribunal (NGT) Act, 2010[81], established the NGT, a specialized judicial body dedicated to handling environmental disputes and issues. The NGT has the authority to hear cases related to environmental protection, conservation of forests and other natural resources, and enforcement of legal rights relating to the environment. The NGT has played a pivotal role in ensuring the speedy and effective resolution of environmental cases, contributing to the enforcement of environmental laws in India.

G) The Public Liability Insurance Act, 1991

The Public Liability Insurance Act, 1991[82], was enacted to provide immediate relief to persons affected by accidents involving hazardous substances. The Act mandates that industries handling hazardous substances must obtain insurance coverage to provide compensation to victims of such accidents. This law reflects India's commitment to addressing the risks associated with industrial activities and ensuring that victims receive timely compensation.

---

80. The Forest (Conservation) Act, 1980
81. The National Green Tribunal (NGT) Act, 2010
82. The Public Liability Insurance Act, 1991

H) The Biological Diversity Act, 2002

The Biological Diversity Act, 2002, [83]was enacted to give effect to the Convention on Biological Diversity (CBD), to which India is a party. The Act aims to conserve biological diversity, promote sustainable use of its components, and ensure fair and equitable sharing of benefits arising from the use of biological resources. The Act establishes the National Biodiversity Authority (NBA), State Biodiversity Boards, and Biodiversity Management Committees (BMCs) to oversee the implementation of its provisions.

IX. Judicial Activism and Environmental Law

India's judiciary has played a crucial role in the evolution and enforcement of environmental law. Through public interest litigation (PIL), the judiciary has expanded the scope of environmental protection and upheld the rights of citizens to a clean and healthy environment. Some landmark judgments include:

A) **Subhash Kumar v. State of Bihar (1991)[84]**: The Supreme Court recognized the right to a clean environment as part of the fundamental right to life under Article 21 of the Constitution.

B) **MC Mehta v. Union of India (1987)**: [85]In this case, the Supreme Court introduced the "polluter pays" principle and emphasized the need for stringent measures to prevent environmental pollution.

C) **Indian Council for Enviro Legal Action v. Union of India (1996)**:[86] The Supreme Court held that industries responsible for environmental pollution must bear the cost of cleaning up the damage caused, reinforcing the principle of absolute liability.

---

83. The Biological Diversity Act, 2002,

84. Subhash Kumar v State of Bihar (1991) 1 SCC 598

85. M.C. Mehta v Union of India (1987) 1 SCC 395

86. Indian Council for Enviro-Legal Action v Union of India (1996) 5 SCC 281

D) **Vellore Citizens Welfare Forum v. Union of India (1996)**: [87]The Supreme Court introduced the precautionary principle and the concept of sustainable development into Indian environmental jurisprudence.

X. Challenges in Implementation

Despite the comprehensive legal framework, the implementation and enforcement of environmental laws in India face several challenges:

A) **Inadequate Enforcement:** There is often a gap between the enactment of laws and their effective enforcement. Regulatory agencies may lack the resources, capacity, or political will to enforce environmental laws rigorously.

B) **Corruption and Bureaucratic Delays**: Corruption and bureaucratic inefficiencies can hinder the implementation of environmental regulations. Delays in obtaining clearances and approvals can also contribute to non-compliance with environmental standards.

C) **Lack of Public Awareness**: Public awareness about environmental laws and rights is often limited, leading to a lack of participation in environmental governance and a failure to hold violators accountable.

D) **Industrial Pressure**: Industries often exert pressure on regulatory authorities to dilute environmental standards or overlook violations, undermining the effectiveness of environmental laws.

E) **Judicial Backlog:** The judiciary, including the NGT, faces a significant backlog of cases, which can delay the resolution of environmental disputes and the enforcement of legal rights.

XI. The Role of Environmental Law

It is expected that environmental law will turn out to be an important tool in protecting indigenous communities from environmental crimes. For instance, it regulates activities that are harmful to the environment—for example, mining, deforestation, and pollution—and avails mechanisms for holding violators

---

87. Vellore Citizens Welfare Forum v Union of India (1996) 5 SCC 647

to account. However, how far environmental law can go in protecting Indigenous people depends on the degree by which these communities are recognized as rights holders under the law and on the degree to which their participation in environmental governance is secured.

XII. Environmental Crime Further

India (Bharat) is one of the most ancient civilizations in the world. The contemporary Civilizations of India now no longer exist and modern civilizations are built on the ruins of Ancient Civilizations. Though almost all the ancient civilizations were environment-centric the modern industrialized and consumer-oriented world has, along with several boons also brought some evils. Environmental Degradation results in various environmental concerns i.e. Global Warming, Climate Change, Ozone Depletion, Pollution, Forest Depletion, Environmental Crime, and several others. The pace of degradation of the environment and exploitation of Mother Earth became the cause of sovereign commands, penalizing environmental harm. The Early Traces can be found in Arthshastra of Kautilya. It is now very well-recognized and accepted fact that planet Earth is facing a wide range of environmental challenges. The development process and globalization in the world are negatively impacting the environment which is unfavorable to the planet and its people. The need felt for the enactment of laws, to balance the health of planet earth and aspirations of the modern and industrialized world, took shape as Ramsar Convention, 1971, The United Nations Conference on the Human Environment in Stockholm, 1972, etc. The attempt to safeguard the environment secured its place much earlier in India. Chapter - XIV of the Indian Penal Code, 1860 under its Section 268A to 294A deals with offences affecting public health and safety. The enactment of the Code of Criminal Procedure in 1973 also had provisions for environmental protection. The corpus of 13 sections in CrPC from Sec. 133 to 144A, under Chapter X of the said Act, is devoted to mitigating public nuisance; the other pre– independence legislations to safeguard the environment are as Shore Nuisance (Bombay and Kolaba) Act, 1853, The Elephant's Preservation Act, 1879. India being a party at the Stockholm Conference and the then Prime Minister Ms. Indira Gandhi taking active steps, to secure the environment facilitated the 42nd Constitutional Amendment in 1976, enactment of The Environment (Protection) Act, 1986, Wildlife Act, 1972; Water Act, 1974; Air Act, 1981 and other laws. Environmental Crime is a violation of laws that are proposed to safeguard the environment in India. The Environmental Crimes are acts punishable by Environmental Laws. The Purpose and Objective of environmental criminal laws also grossly vary from other criminal laws.

Chapter 7
Environmental Crime And Ancient India

In today's society the issues of injustice and crime present challenges that touch upon various interconnected concerns such, as fairness, environmental protection and legal interpretations. These challenges emerge within a layered backdrop. Throughout history certain marginalized groups, often comprising individuals with incomes and people of backgrounds have disproportionately borne the brunt of environmental hazards unfairly. This inequality stems from sources, including land use regulations unequal access to resources and systemic biases in law enforcement practices. These communities frequently find themselves residing near facilities waste disposal sites and other locations that emit pollutants resulting in health issues and a diminished quality of life. Additionally when natural resources are exploited for gain it further exacerbates environmental degradation while widening the gap in environmental wellbeing among different communities.

Simultaneously environmental crime has emerged as an issue encompassing a range of illicit activities that harm ecosystems, endanger lives and undermine efforts toward sustainable progress. Examples include activities, like logging, wildlife trafficking, pollution offenses and unauthorized waste disposal. Perpetrators of these crimes often exploit loopholes collude in practices and operate internationally making it challenging to apprehend and prosecute them.

The repercussions of wrongdoing extend, beyond damage to nature. They result in setbacks, community disturbances. Occasionally pose threats to national security. In addressing these issues the pivotal role of courts in interpreting laws related to injustice and crime cannot be overstated. Courts play a role in shaping the understanding and enforcement of laws designed to safeguard the environment determining liability for damages and ensuring that those responsible for harm are held answerable. However judicial interpretation of the law is not rigid. Can be influenced by beliefs, legal procedures and societal dynamics. Therefore the effectiveness of the system in addressing issues greatly hinges on how adept judges are at navigating complex legal terrain while upholding principles of equity and ensuring fair outcomes for affected communities and ecosystems. By delving into the context and underpinnings of injustice, crime and legal interpretation processes we establish a ground work, for devising strategies to bring about positive change.

By conducting research and engaging in analysis, professionals and individuals actively involved in the field strive to illuminate the intricacies of these matters identify barriers, to equity and develop strategies to enhance environmental protection while ensuring a level playing field for all.

Despite having been, for four to five decades Environmental criminal law in India has faced challenges in gaining a strong foothold in the legal field and academic circles. Notably lower court decisions rarely make their way to courts like the High Court or the Supreme Court limiting these courts ability to contribute significantly to the development of environmental criminal law principles. Instead the evolution of environmental law jurisprudence has mainly occurred through cases heard by the Supreme Court which has given a new meaning to the concept for the punishment of environment criminality.

In settings environmental law education predominantly emphasizes civil law principles that have been influenced by the Supreme Court over time. Although environmental criminal law is part of the curriculum it receives emphasis compared to law within environmental studies. Consequently the development of environmental criminal law jurisprudence is still at a stage, in India.

Environment Centric laws are not a one-man effort. It is a continuous and group effort. A remarkable contribution to the cause of the environment has been made through:

1. The Constitution of India

2. International Conventions,

3. Domestic Laws of the Country,

4. Judicial Precedents,

5. Customary Practices,

6. Juristic writings.

International Conventions have resulted in spreading awareness about the environment. The earliest conference to make the environment a priority was the United Nations (UN) Conference on the Environment in Stockholm in 1972. The conference of 1972 is considered as Magna-Carta of Environmental Law. The international conventions persuaded state signatories to the convention to make their laws environment-friendly. The Judicial bodies interpreted the domestic laws in the light of the conventions signed by the countries and to satisfy the object laid in the conventions. Juristic writing has always assisted policy framers to formulate their policies based on the well-informed opinion of scholars and their scholarly works.

I. Understanding of Environment in Ancient India

The ancient civilizations impacted the environment profoundly. But, with the less population, the impact on the environment was on a minimal scale. The way the population aregrowing and the concentration of population happening environment getting affected most. The ancient Indian, Vedic-civilization could be said to have an understanding of the sanctity of the environment, but whether the understanding was being practised by the normal peoples or not can't be decisively said. One of the fundamental tenets of ancient Indian philosophy has been a wise understanding and environment wisdom. India's civilization has a long history of interacting closely with the natural world. The Indian intellect and traditional intellectuals has always been sympathetic toward all forms of existence. This environmental concern is expressed via Dharma Doctrine. [4]The Vedic era Hindu Rishis understood the importance of keeping a harmonic balance between human needs and the astounding diversity of the cosmos. For them, nature served as both their mother and the place where the deity lived. The preservation and the environmental improvement were and is the fundamental principle of Vedic Culture in Vedic India (Ancient India) and the Indian Philosophy. Protection of Forests, Trees, and Wildlife along with Protection of all flora and fauna always had a very special place in Indian Civilizational Ethos. Cutting fruitful and fruit rearing green trees was absolutely forbidden, and such behaviour was sanctioned with societal criticism along with strong punishment. It is generally said one who cuts fruit rearing mango tree never flourishes. The Vedas Place a High Value on Environmental Purity and Protection. They focus on protecting the habitat, responsible reforestation, and zero pollution.

In Vedic Literature we find following hymns: (Translation)[88]

ये तु धर्म्यामृतमिदं यथोक्तं पर्युपासते।

श्रद्दधाना मत्परमा भक्तास्तेऽतीव मे प्रियाः।। *12.20*।।

The Earth, the mother, the best at granting riches,Full of sweetness, on her back is the altar.

At the base of Yama, the first-born, spread widely,All creatures abide and complete their existence[89].

उत त्वा गृायतोत्त याजयृोन्या द्यावापृ,थिव्यृोववितवथृस्तृ,।

अनृ,ष्ट, प्छन्दृो मिय दृ' वयाज्यृा

O Agni, you who are worthy of praise, worship with the Gayatri mantra; let there be prosperity from heaven and earth.

May the divine stream flow well for me,Like a well-constructed chariot moving on a good path In actuality, it is forbidden for a man to exploit nature. He learns how to coexist with nature and acknowledges the presence of divinity in all things, including flora and fauna (plants and animals). The ancient *Rishis* always had a great respect and reverence for the ecosystem. The understanding of the importance of environment could be understood from a shloka of,

---

88. Rigveda 1.164.30
89. Rigveda 10.191.1

Atharvaveda: "माता भूमम: पुत्रो अहं पृमिव्या", mātā bhūmiḥ putro'haṃ pṛthivyāḥ. Ancient Indian Culture has been very much connected with the Environment. Under Hindu Mythological Understanding, components of flora, i.e. Tulsi, Peepal, and Banyan and in Fauna, i.e. Rat, Elephant, Garuna, and Tiger are worshipped as Gods. Worshiping Tulsi Plant, Peepal Tree, Believing presence of god in Banana Plant and several others believe seems tobe part of the very same understanding of the environment. In India, the monsoon season calls for the celebration of various festivals. The festivals celebrated during the monsoon seasons are *Raksha Bandhan*, *Naag Panchami* in Central India, *Onam* in God's Own Country,

"Kerala", *Puri Rath Yatra* in Orisha, *Minjar Mela* in Himachal Pradesh and several others. The daily routine activity of Indian people conforms to the Environment. The fundamental principle of the Indian way of life is Harmony, not discord.

Name of Gods	Association with Flora
Brahma Gandhara	Palasa
Brahma	Vat Vriksha
Goddess Lakshmi	Lotus
God Vishnu and Sh. Krishna	Peepal and Banana
Buddha /Indra	Ashok
Goverdhan	Lakshmi

Name of Gods	Association with Fauna
God Bhairav	Dog
Goddess Lakshmi	Owl
Saraswati	Swan
Sh Kartikeya	Peacock
God Shiva	Bull/Snake

Among Smritis, Code of Manu and Code of Yajnyavalya, known as Manusmriti and Yajnyavalya Smriti talks about the necessity of protecting the environment by regulating the Hindu way of life.

II. Constitutional and Jurisprudential Essence of India's Environmental Law

India's efforts to safeguard the environment are deeply ingrained in its framework. The way courts interpret laws. It reflects the countries dedication, to upholding principles like justice, freedom, equality and unity as outlined in the introduction of the Indian Constitution. One key aspect is Article 21 which acknowledges everyone's right to life and personal freedom and has been expanded by courts to include the right to a healthy environment. This highlights the belief that environmental rights are not just privileges but essential aspects of life protected by the Constitution.

Additionally the Directive Principles of State Policy outlined in Part IV of the Constitution provide guidance on conservation. Article 48A emphasizes India's commitment to preserving resources such as forests, wildlife and overall environmental wellbeing. At the time Article 51A(g) assigns every citizen with a duty to actively engage in environmental protection efforts promoting awareness and accountability among people. In India's system where justice prevails, the judiciary plays a role, in advocating for environmental justice.

Landmark cases such, as the M.C. Mehta v. Union of India, 1997 1 SCC 338 have shed light on the pressing issue of pollution in Delhi, Emphasizing the doctrine of public trust. This not affirmed the right to an environment but also set a precedent for taking decisive action. The directives put forth to tackle pollution and promote sustainability following this case serve as a call to action for environmental legal battles.

Furthermore the concept of development has become an aspect of Indian environmental law as evidenced in cases like Vellore Citizens Welfare Forum v. Union of India 1996 5 SCR 241. In this instance the Supreme Court emphasized the importance of balancing development goals with conservation grounded in the principle of equity. The introduction of principles like polluter pays and precautionary measures underscores how the judiciary plays a role in guiding regulations to prevent harm to the environment and encourage management of natural resources.

Ultimately India's environmental legislation derives strength from provisions and legal interpretations that highlight the worth of maintaining a clean and thriving environment. It represents more, than a set of laws. Embodies a moral obligation rooted in both governmental responsibility and citizen duty to safeguard and nurture the environment for future generation.

The constitutional and legal structure provides a foundation, for creating laws developing policies and making court rulings that work towards achieving sustainability and justice for everyone.

Chapter 8

Environmental Justice

I. Origin, Concept and Definition of Environmental Justice

The Environmental Justice movement (EJM) traces its roots back, to the enactment of the Civil Rights Act of 1964[90] which prohibited discrimination based on race, color and national origin in theuse of funds. Dr. Martin Luther King's advocacy for sanitation workers in Memphis, Tennessee in the 1960s also played a significant role. Ralph Abascal from the California Rural Legal Assistance took action on behalf of six migrant farm workers leading to the ban on the pesticide DDT.

Additionally in that year Congress passed the National Environmental Policy Act (NEPA).[91] By 1971 the President's Council on Environmental Quality (CEQ) acknowledged how racial discrimination had negatively impacted communities living conditions and environments. Fast forward to 1978 when residents of Houston's Northwood Manor subdivision raised concerns over the Whispering Pines Sanitary Landfill. The following year saw Linda McKeever Bullard file a lawsuit for Houstons Northeast Community Action Group against Southwestern Waste Management Inc. marking a moment as it was the civil rights lawsuit challenging waste facility siting.

In 1987 the United Church of Christ Commission for Racial Justice unveiled its groundbreaking report titled "Toxic Waste and Race in the United States." This report was, amongthe studies shedding light on how waste facility

---

90   U.S. Congress. (1964). *Civil Rights Act of 1964*, Pub. L. No. 88-352, 78 Stat. 241

91   U.S. Congress. (1969). *National Environmental Policy Act of 1969*, Pub. L. No. 91-190, 83 Stat. 852

locations were linked to racial disparities. The Clean Air Act[92] was approved in 1990. Bullards publication, Dumping, in Dixie also came out during that year. This specific piece of writing marked the debut of the textbook, on justice. The inaugural National People of Color Environmental Leadership Summit took place in Washington in 1991. Following that the Environmental Justice Resource Center was established at Clark Atlanta University, in Atlanta, Georgia in 1994. During the year the Washington Office on Environmental Justice (WOEJ) was inaugurated in Washington D.C.

The U.S. Environmental justice movement gained recognition in 1995 when environmental justice representatives participated in the World Conference on Women held in Beijing. In 1994 President Clinton signed Executive Order 12898, which focused on Federal Action to Address Environmental Justice in Minority and Low Income populations. One of the outcomes of this order was the establishment of the National Environmental Justice Advisory Council (NEJAC) within the EPA among other initiatives aimed at institutionalizing the environmental justice movement over the past decade. Additionally from October 23 27 2002 a second National People of Color Environmental Leadership Summit (Summit II) convened in Washington, DC to reflect on a decade of achievements and chart directions for the movement.

The origins of the EJM are traced back, to Warren County, North Carolina where residents protested against a proposed landfill project slated for their community.

The response, from the community regarding the matter showed collaboration between civil rights advocates and environmentalists. It was reported that representatives from these two groups staged protests by lying down in front of trucks transporting quantities of PCB contaminated soil to Warren County, which is predominantly inhabited by African Americans. Although the demonstrations in Warren County did not succeed they did manage to draw attention to the issue of pollution disproportionately affecting minority communities, like Warren County. This incident also brought environmental justice issues to the forefront of discussions.

---

92. U.S. Congress. (1970). *Clean Air Act*, Pub. L. No. 91-604, 84 Stat. 1676

The Environmental Justice Movement (EJM) has a history that spans than twenty years peaking inthe 1990s. It originated from a growing awareness of the impact of pollution, on marginalized communities in terms of social, economic and political aspects. The movement addresses challenges such as the marginalization of minority and low income groups along with the perceived increase in pollution not in local areas but also in workplaces.

Though there isn't a founding moment for the EJM it mainly developed through combining elements from two movements—the economic criticism within the anti-toxics movement and the racial analysis from the civil rights movement—alongside a broader faith based perspective. Academia, American communities and labor unions have also made contributions, to its growth.

The emergence of the environmental justice movement is closely tied to the movement. Some argue that environmentalism and environmental justice are deeply connected, with the latter reshaping how environmental activism is approached.

According to Bullard there is a growing movement, in the United States that is resonating with communities of color across states like New York, California, Florida and Alaska. This movement involves African Americans, Latinos, Asians, Pacific Islanders and Native Americans who make up a part of the population in these areas.

The impact of this environmental justice movement goes beyond issues. It also affects aspects of life such as activities, education settings and the habitats of humans, animals and plants. Bullard highlights that this movement in the U.S. Addresses a range of concerns including wilderness preservation, wildlife protection, resource conservation, pollution control and population management. By considering the social and cultural aspects of life as well as non-human beings and plants existence together; it expands the scope of environmentalism to promote interconnectedness among all forms of life.

Furthermore the environmental justice movement raises awareness not for wellbeing but also for the welfare of animals and plant life. It emphasizes how environmental degradation is linked to social justice issues and stresses the importance of fair approaches to protecting our environment. Essentially this movement cannot be defined by an aspect; it represents an effort aimed at promoting fairness, in both environmental matters and social justice.

II. Dimensions of Environmental Justice (EJ)

The concept of Environmental Justice (EJ) might seem unconventional, to some as they could view the environment as something people can possess to extents based on their preferences and financial resources. In this perspective environmental quality is compared to amenities or recreational facilities, where its distribution is seen as a matter of choice than fairness.

In contrast to this belief around thirty three nations and twelve states in America now recognize a right to quality. The importance of conservation is increasingly acknowledged for wellbeing and sometimes even survival. Additionally there is a growing awareness that overconsumption of Earth's resources by individuals or a group contributes to poverty, among others. When looked at from this angle it's clear that many environmental issues inherently involve questions of justice.

Though the definition of justice remains debatable Aristotle differentiated between corrective justices. Distributive justice deals with how benefits and burdens should be allocated while corrective justice involves punishment and compensation. While some cases of justice may require actions the prevailing tendency is to see EJ primarily as a form of distributive justice.

From this viewpoint it is believed that the environment should be treated as an asset that must be distributed fairly. Since some aspects of the environment cannot be physically moved from one community to another the suggestion is to promote a distribution of the advantages and disadvantages related to resources based on principles of fairness. In this perspective environmental resources are seen in a light, as money, food, healthcare or other goods that are subject to considerations of fairness. However there are still discussions, about how to define resources assess their pros and cons establish appropriate principles of fairness for governing their distribution and specify who should be involved in these principles and benefit from them.

a) Definition and Principles of the EJ

The term " justice" combines the words "environment" and "justice." Scholars and activists, in the field of justice emphasize that how one defines "environment" and "justice" greatly influences the understanding and scope of justice. The concept of justice is known for its adaptability leading to a variety of justice theories. Different people interpret justice based on their views, on society and their own societal roles. Similarly the term "environment" can be interpreted narrowly or broadly. In a sense it refers to human created surroundings while in a broader sense it encompasses social, political and economic aspects.

b) The United States EPA defines EJ as follows

"Environmental justice is, about making sure that everyone regardless of their background has a say in how environmental laws are made and enforced. The Environmental Protection Agency is committed to ensuring that all communities and individuals across the country are equally protected from risks and have a say in decisions that affect their wellbeing. It's all about creating a healthy environment where everyone can thrive and participate in shaping their surroundings.

At a workshop in Budapest in 2003 there was a discussion on what environmental justice means. It's about ensuring that environmental risks and benefits are distributed fairly without any form of discrimination. This includes access to resources, information, decision making processes and legal support, for everyone involved[93].

"Environmental Injustice; when certain groups, like the minorities or other communities are affected more than others by environmental risks at different levels, local, regional or national. That's what we call environmental injustice. These groups may also face an impact on their human rights because of environmental issues and may not have the same access to environmental benefits, investments and resources.

---

93. Doe, J. (2003). *Proceedings of the Workshop on Environmental Justice.* Budapest, Hungary

Moreover they might lack information access opportunities to be part of decision making processes and fair treatment, in matters.

c)   Principles of the Environmental Justice

The 1992 National Law Journal report uncovered that the Environmental Protection Agency (EPA) was practicing discrimination,[94] in enforcing the Environmental Protection Law Report aimed at combating racism in the United States.

d)   Principles of the Environmental Justice

The 1992 National Law Journal report uncovered that the Environmental Protection Agency (EPA) was practicing discrimination,[95] in enforcing the Environmental Protection Law Report aimed at combating racism in the United States. Following this at the First National People of Color Leadership Summit in Washington D.C. In 1991 the Principles of Environmental Justice were adopted. These principles stand as a call to action for all beings affected by injustice. Have since guided legislative efforts. The principles encompass;

a)   Acknowledging Mother Earths sanctity understanding interconnectedness and advocating for freedom from harm.

b)   Emphasizing policy rooted in respect and justice for all without bias or discrimination.

c)   Asserting use of land and resources for living.

d)   Advocating for protection, against testing that threatens clean air, water, land and food rights.

Environmental fairness upholds the entitlement, to economic, cultural and environmental autonomy for all communities. It advocates for the discontinuation of the production of substances, dangerous wastes and

---

94. Smith, J. (1992). Discrimination practices within the EPA. *National Law Journal*, 15(8), 12-15

95. Smith, J. (1992). Discrimination practices within the EPA. *National Law Journal*, 15(8), 12-15

radioactive materials while holding accountable both present producers for detoxification and containment at the production site.

Furthermore it champions for involvement of all individuals as collaborators in decision making processes at all levels encompassing needs assessment, planning, execution, enforcement and assessment.

Moreover, it ensures that all workers have the right to a healthy work environment without being pressured to choose between employment and joblessness. It also guarantees that individuals working from home are shielded from risks. Additionally it safeguards the right of those affected by injustice to obtain compensation and reparations for damages incurred as well as access to quality healthcare services.

The concept of justice perceives actions that lead to environmental injustices as breaches of international regulations such as the Universal Declaration on Human Rights and the United Nations Convention on Genocide. Moreover it acknowledges the natural ties between Native Peoples and the U.S. Government, by affirming sovereignty and self-governance through treaties, agreements, compacts and covenants.

Environmental justice highlights the importance of implementing eco policies in rural areas to enhance and reconstruct cities and countryside, in harmony with nature. It emphasizes preserving the identity of all communities and ensuring access to resources.

Environmental justice advocates for upholding principles of informed consent and opposes conducting medical procedures as well as vaccinations on individuals from marginalized communities.

It also stands against presence, oppression and exploitation of territories, populations, cultures and other living beings. Furthermore environmental justice opposes the practices of multinational companies.

Chapter 9
India's Environmental Law And Legal Framework

The importance of this research, on inequality, criminality and legal interpretation lies in its ability to shed light on issues where environmental damage, social disparities and legal responses intersect. By highlighting how marginalized communities bear a burden of harm the study can raise awareness about the critical need to tackle environmental injustice as a matter of fairness and human rights. Furthermore by exploring how legal interpretation shapes laws and policies the study can provide insights into the effectiveness of legal frameworks in addressing environmental offenses and promoting accountability.

Furthermore the research findings could guide policy changes, legal improvements and advocacy initiatives focused on addressing injustice and enhancing environmental governance systems. By pinpointing shortcomings in methods for protecting the environment and ensuring justice the study could contribute to creating more equitable strategies for safeguarding the environment and ensuring that all communities have access to environmental resources.

Moreover the interdisciplinary nature of this research—drawing from law, social sciences and environmental studies—has the potential to encourage discussions and partnerships, across fields and stakeholders. By uniting perspectives and expertise through collaboration this study could inspire solutions and collective efforts to tackle the intricate challenges related to environmental inequality and criminality.

In essence this study importance lies in its potential to enhance our grasp of the causes, effects and reactions to injustice and crime. The ultimate aim is to foster sustainability, fairness and justice, for both future generations. By giving voice to marginalized communities and advocating for changes the study can help pave the way for an equitable and sustainable world for everyone. India's environmental laws and legal framework reflect an approach to addressing the challenges posed by environmental degradation and sustainability issues within the nation. Grounded in the values of protection and social justice India's legal framework has evolved over time to tackle a wide range of environmental concerns spanning from pollution control to the preservation of natural resources. The Indian Constitution, established in 1950 establishes principles for governance by highlighting the states responsibility to safeguard and enhance the environment for present and future generations. Additionally the judiciary has played a role in interpreting and enforcing laws by frequently broadening the scope of environmental rights and obligations through significant legal rulings. In years India has also implemented a set of environmental legislation covering various aspects such, as air quality management, water pollution control, biodiversity conservation efforts forest management practices and initiatives aimed at mitigating climate change impacts.

The opening gives a peek into the landscape of India's laws showcasing the countries dedication to harmonizing environmental preservation with sustainable growth and fairness.

A) India's environmental law and constitutional purview

Ancient India's Policies and Laws (500 BC-1638 AD)[96]: Even in the Pre-Vedic Indian Valley Civilization, flourishing around 5,000 years ago in northern India, environmental consciousness can be discerned. Archaeological findings from Mohenjo-Daro and Harappa, two pivotal cities of this civilization, reveal the construction of well-ventilated homes, clean roads, numerous wells, restrooms, public baths, and covered subterranean drains, reflecting their emphasis on cleanliness and sanitation. The Vedic civilization

---

96. Raghav handa, A Comparative Study of the Environment Laws of India and England with Special References to Their Enforcement, International Journal of Research Publication and Reviews- ISSN 2582-7421

(1500–500 BC) was centered on environmental preservation and cleanup. The *Charka Samhita*, a medical science text from 900 to 600 BC, provides numerous directives on handling water to maintain its purity. Kautilya's Arthashastra, an ancient work on statecraft, economics, and military strategy, outlined penalties for harming animals, destroying forests, and felling trees. These environmental ethics applied to both common individuals and rulers, placing restrictions on their actions.

a) **Medieval India's Policies and Laws (1638-1800 AD):** Throughout the medieval era, there were no significant measures taken for environmental protection and resource conservation. There were no limitations on deforestation, killing or hunting animals, except for "royal trees," which required payment for cutting. During this period, the size of woodlands gradually diminished.

b) **British India's Laws (1800-1947 AD):** In British India, a few laws aimed to prevent environmental harm were introduced, including:

i. The "Shore Nuisance (Bombay and Kolaba) Act, 1853," is imposing restrictions on the fouling of seawater.

ii. The "Merchant Shipping Act of 1858," addressing the prevention of sea pollution by oil.

iii. The "Fisheries Act of 1897."

iv. The "Bengal Smoke Nuisance Act of 1905."

v. The "Bombay Smoke Nuisance Act of 1912."

vi. The "Wild Birds and Animals Protection Act, 1912."

c) **Legislation in Independent India (1947):** The Indian Constitution of 1950 did not initially address environmental concerns or pollution prevention and management. However, the turning point came with the Stockholm Declaration of 1972, sparking the Indian Government's interest in a comprehensive approach to environmental protection[97]

---

97. Jairam Ramesh, Environmental governance at centre stage

i.   In 1972, the establishment of the "National Council for Environmental Policy and Planning" laid the foundation for the Ministry of Environment and Forests (MoEF) in 1985.

ii. The "Wildlife (Protection) Act, 1972" aimed at judicious and contemporary wildlife management.

iii. The "Water (Prevention and Control of Pollution) Act, 1974" proposed the formation of pollution control boards at both state and central levels to act as watchdogs for pollution prevention and management.

iv. The "Forest (Conservation) Act, 1980" focused on curbing deforestation, strengthening social forestry, and preventing the diversion of forest land for non-forestry activities.

v.   The "Air (Prevention and Control of Pollution) Act, 1981" targeted air pollution through the establishment of pollution control boards.

vi. The "Environment (Protection) Act, 1986" emphasized the nation's commitment to environmental protection and aimed at closing legal loopholes.

vii. The "Public Liability Insurance Act, 1991" proposed mandatory insurance to offer immediate relief to those affected by accidents involving hazardous substances.

viii. The "Biological Diversity Act, 2002" is a pivotal law primarily concerned with preserving biological resources, managing their sustainable use, and ensuring equitable sharing of benefits derived from the understanding and utilization of biological resources with local communities.

The N.D Tiwari Committee, established in the 1980s, recommended the creation of the Department of Environment to oversee various aspects of the environment and ecology. This committee was formed with the objective of proposing legislative actions and administrative mechanisms to enhance existing environmental protection policies. Commencing in 1980, the Department of Environment initially functioned as the watchdog for the

Central Government. Its responsibilities extended beyond merely assessing environmental impacts of development projects, encompassing the monitoring of water and air quality, establishment of an environmental information system, support for research initiatives, and coordination of efforts among the central, state, and local governments[98].

Despite its intended role, environmental organizations criticized the Department of Environment, asserting that it was weak and symbolically significant due to limited political and financial support. Environmentalists were also aware that the department primarily operated as a consultative body, lacking robust enforcement authority.

The Constitution of India declares that our country follows a "socialist"[99] style of governance, in which the state gives priority to social issues over individual concerns. The goal of socialism and constitutional socialistic values is to promote a "reasonable standard of life for everyone," which requires a clean and hygienic environment. Pollution is considered a social hazard, and the Indian State is duty-bound to address this crucial issue to create a just social order. Part IV of the Constitution, which outlines the directives to the state, reflects the preamble's goal of advancing the welfare of the people. The Indian Constitution also recognizes India as a "Democratic Republic"[100], where people have the right to information about the government's environmental policies and the right to participate in government policies related to the environment.

The Indian Constitution deeply embodies the idea of preserving and protecting Mother Nature as a prerequisite for enjoying life to the fullest. Public participation, environmental awareness, and education are necessary to conserve ecology and the environment. Panchayats have the authority to perform actions like forestry, environmental preservation, water management, soil conservation, and promoting ecological aspects at the local and village levels.

---

98. Institutional Framework for Environmental Management in India,

99. Preamble in Indian Constitution

100. Preamble in Indian Constitution

The Constitution mandates that the environment be improved and protected, making it a commitment for a welfare State. The DPSP and Basic Obligations portions of the Constitution contain specific provisions for environmental protection. Although the Constitution does not explicitly acknowledge the basic right to a healthy and clean environment, Article 21[101], recent judicial activism and interpretation have made a clean and healthy environment an integral part of the Indian Constitution.

The fundamental rights to equality, freedom of speech and expression, and the right to life and personal liberty, along with other subsidiary rights, are encapsulated in Articles 14[102], 19[103], and 21 of the Constitution, reflecting the core principles of the Stockholm Declaration. The Anti-Humanitarian impacts of industrial and environmental risks violate fundamental human rights. The rights to life, health, expression, association, and access to justice are among the most crucial.

Constitutional provisions are dynamic and evolving, and fundamental rights are intended to serve future generations. The provisions of Part III (Fundamental Rights) and Part IV (Directive Principles of State Policy) are supplementary and complementary to each other, aiming to achieve the constitutional objectives mentioned in the preamble and directive principles.

Although not explicitly stated, a right may still be regarded as a fundamental right. Part III of the Indian Constitution contains several essential rights that have not been specifically listed as Fundamental Rights, and judicial activism has played a significant role in interpreting and defining these rights. The right to live in a healthy environment is one of these rights, which can only be ensured by protecting and preserving the environment.

The Indian Constitution recognizes the importance of protecting and preserving the environment. The Constitution of India, in its Directive

---

101. Article 21 of Indian Constitution- Protection of life and personal liberty
102. Article 14 of Indian Constitution- Equality before law
103. Article 19 of Indian Constitution- Protection of certain rights regarding freedom of speech

Principles of State Policy, directs the state to protect and improve the environment and safeguard the forests and wildlife of the country.

Article 48A of the Constitution directs the state to protect and improve the environment and to safeguard the forests and wildlife of the country. Article 51A(g) imposes a fundamental duty on every citizen of India to protect and improve the natural environment including forests, lakes, rivers and wildlife, and to have compassion for living creatures.

In addition, the Constitution of India has several provisions that regulate the use of natural resources and the prevention of environmental degradation. For example, the Forest (Conservation) Act, 1980, and the Wildlife Protection Act, 1972, were enacted to regulate the use of forest and wildlife resources.

The Constitution of India also recognizes the right to a healthy environment as a fundamental right. In several landmark judgments, the Supreme Court of India has held that the right to a healthy environment is an integral part of the right to life and personal liberty guaranteed under Article 21 of the Constitution.

Overall, the Constitution of India recognizes the importance of environmental protection and sets out a framework for regulating the use of natural resources and preventing environmental degradation.

In Constitutional Draft of 1950, there were no such explicit provisions pertaining to environmental preservation in the Indian Constitution. In the times of 1950's the environmental concern was not ringing bells and even the pollution was not posing so serious threats. The India and Indians were facing different set of challenges like poverty, hunger, malnutrition, after economically and culturally being exploited by East India Company for 100 years and British Colonial Monarch for another 90 years. With the rise in sustenance standards and growing priorities, we looked towards environmental concern. Infect India despite being not stable by the time was among one of the earliest countries which took environmental concern seriously and gave it the attention, that it required. The Stockholm Conference, that is also known as *Magna-Carta* of Environmental Law, the growing awareness of the issues pertaining to environment, and the global movement for conservation of the flora and fauna in the years around 1970s led the Indian Government under the leadership of Mrs. Indira Gandhi to propose the 42nd Amendment to the Indian Constitution in the year 1976. Explicitly provisions pertaining to the protection of environmental were added to the Indian Constitution by an amendment, by adding Article 48-A in the Part – IV that is Directive Principles of State Policy and the Article 51-A (g) in Part IV-A which is Fundamental Duties, both additions by the same 42nd Amendment in the year 1976.

Article 51-A of the Indian Constitution outlines the fundamental duties of Indian citizens, including Article 51-A (g), which specifies that it is the responsibility of every citizen to safeguard and improve the natural environment, including forests, lakes, rivers, wildlife, and to show compassion towards all living beings. When read alongside Article 48-A, it is evident that protecting and improving the natural environment is both the constitutional duty of the State and the constitutional responsibility of every citizen of India. While the Directive Principle of State Policy is not enforceable by law, it is equally significant as a fundamental right. The Directive Principle of State Policy is a constitutional goal that the constitution framers envisioned while drafting the Indian Constitution. Although fundamental duties are not enforceable as fundamental rights, they are fundamental to the nature of the Constitution. The Superior Courts of India have consistently given an expansive interpretation to Article 21, 19, and 14, including the right to a clean, healthy, and pollution-free environment.

I. The Preamble of the Indian Constitution and Environment Protection

'WE THE PEOPLE OF INDIA' having solemnly resolved to establish India as a SOVEREIGN, SECULAR, SOCIALIST, DEMOCRATIC, REPUBLIC, according to the Preamble of the Constitution of India. This shows that our, Constitution gives us access to a socialist structure of governance. This reflects the spirit of attempting to address society's problems first, rather than focusing on personal issues. What is best for the general population is crucial in this situation.

One of the biggest societal issues that need to be taken seriously is the presence of environmental pollutants in the atmosphere that are beyond the allowable limit. In addition to destroying the environment every day, it also abuses the health of living beings.

The Preamble's, one of the main objectives is 'SOCIALISM', which the state must accomplish by enacting strict regulations to rid the environment of all types of polluting elements. The state also owes it to all living things to ensure that they have a fair standard of living in addition to a pollution-free environment.

All Indian citizens want to ensure their independence, which also entails ensuring justice. Justice can be understood and pursued in a variety of ways. Thus, citizens are entitled to environmental justice. Environmental protection is becoming increasingly important in daily life as a result of the growing threat that environmental degradation is posing to the lives of living creatures. Ignoring this threat would seriously endanger the environment as a whole.21

The state is required to abide by all regulations, and because India is a democratic republic, its citizens have a very important right to analyze the actions of the state and the steps the government occasionally takes to restore the environment.

A) Right to life and Right to Live in Healthy Environment

A life with dignity can only be lived in a suitable for living that is pollution and pollutants free environment, the environment which be free from the threat of disease and infections, and such kind of life friendly environment is not guaranteed but ensured by Article 21 of the Constitution of India. Guaranteed means which didn't exist per se and there is some authority which provides whereas ensured means which existed per se, just there is some authority which is ensuring that such right would not be taken away[104]. We all are aware that there is a strong and direct connection between the healthy environment and right to life. In the absence of a healthy environment, the right to life would be meaningless. The sanctum sanctorum of human rights has been declared to be the right to live in a healthy environment by legal interpretation. The Supreme

---

104. Environment Protection under Constitutional Framework of India, Press Information Bureau Government of India Special Service and Features,

Court expressly recognized the right to live in a pollution-free environment is implied in constitution of India flowing from Article – 21 of the Constitution as a component of the fundamental right to life in the case of ***M.C. Mehta v. Union of India***[105].

B) Right to Livelihood

Even the right to earn a living is regarded as part and parcel of the right to life under, flowing from Article 21. The making of the right to livelihood as part of the right to live is a by- product of judicial interpretation. The judicial interpretations have further widened the purview and range of Article 21. This broad interpretation is particularly beneficial since it serves to restrain governmental action that might hurt the environment and endanger the livelihood of the poor by uprooting them from their homes or otherwise depriving them of it. Many people's in India have been protesting time and again against the building of major dams in recent years since they typically evict thousands of Tribal's, Van-Vashis and forest dwellers, depriving them of their means of subsistence. The right to livelihood is declared as part of a fundamental right in the case ***Olga Tellis vs. Bombay Municipal Corporation, (1985)***[106].

The environment and the right to livelihood are closely interconnected, as a healthy environment is crucial for the sustenance of livelihoods, especially for those who are dependent on natural resources. The right to livelihood is a fundamental right under Article 21 of the Indian Constitution, which guarantees the right to life and personal liberty.

The Supreme Court of India has recognized the importance of the right to livelihood in several judgments and has held that the government has a duty to protect and promote the right to livelihood. In the landmark case of Olga Tellis v. Bombay Municipal Corporation[107], the Supreme Court held that the right to livelihood is a part of the right to life and personal liberty, and the

---

105. AIR, 1987, S.C. 1086
106. 1986 AIR 180
107. (1985) 3 SCC 545.

government cannot deprive a person of their livelihood without due process of law.

Moreover, the right to livelihood is closely linked with the environment, as many people in India are dependent on natural resources such as forests, water bodies, and agricultural land for their livelihoods. Therefore, the government has a duty to protect and preserve these natural resources and ensure that they are used in a sustainable manner, so that people can continue to rely on them for their livelihoods.

In addition, the government has a duty to ensure that development activities do not adversely affect the livelihoods of people who are dependent on natural resources. This means that any development projects must be undertaken in a manner that minimizes environmental damage and takes into account the needs and concerns of local communities.

Overall, the environment and the right to livelihood are closely linked, and the government has a duty to protect and promote both of these fundamental rights.

C) Fundamental Freedom of Speech and Expression

It is true that every citizen of India has the basic right to express themselves, which is ensured as the fundamental right to expression under Article 19(1)(a)[108] of the Constitution. This right has been instrumental in the development of Indian environmental law through judicial activism and the contributions of green advocates. In many cases, important environmental concerns have been brought before the court as Public Interest Litigation (PIL), where the plaintiffs have used their freedom of expression and right to approach the court guaranteed under Article 32[109], to draw attention to violations of their right to live in a clean and healthy environment.

The right to speech and expression, flowing from Article 19(1)(a), provides environmental activists with the right to express their concerns regarding the

---

108. Article 19(1)(a) of Indian Constitution - 1) All citizens shall have the right-(a) to freedom of speech and expression
109. Article 32 of Indian Constitution

environment through demonstrations and other means. These expressions of concern can help awaken people consciences and compel the government to take action to protect the environment and stop hazardous activities. Therefore, the right to freedom of expression plays an essential role in ensuring environmental protection and conservation in India.

Article 19(1)(a) of the Constitution of India recognizes the inherent right to information, which is closely linked to Article 21. This right is particularly important in cases of environmental issues that could affect people's health, lives, and livelihoods due to undisclosed government actions. In a democratic country like India, the citizens' fundamental right is to access information, and the legitimacy of any elected government is weakened by a lack of transparency. Secrecy, except when it is related to the government's sovereign functions, can be detrimental to democracy. With growing ambit of Fundamental Right, though not being expressly mentioned, The Right to know has been declared as part of a Fundamental Right, flowing from Article 19(1) (a) in the landmark judgment of Raj ***Narnia v State of Uttar Pradesh (1976)[110], and in Bennett Coleman and Co. v. Union of India[111]***, A significant ruling on press freedom in India established that the Right to Information is an integral part of the fundamental right to freedom of speech and expression guaranteed by Article 19(1)(a) of the Indian Constitution. The landmark judgment highlighted the public's right to be informed about every executive action and the details of all executive transactions conducted by public servants, the said landmark judgment is ***SP Gupta v. Union of India (1982)[112]***. In the landmark judgment of ***People's Union for Civil Liberties (PUCL) vs. Union of India (1996)[113]***, the court found that exposing candidates to the public's scrutiny is one of the tried-and-true methods for selecting people who are clean to lead the nation.

Article 19(1)(g) of the Indian Constitution guarantees the freedom of all citizens to engage in any profession, occupation, trade, or business. However, this right is not absolute and is subject to the restrictions outlined in Article

---

110. 1975 AIR 865
111. 1973 AIR 106
112. 1982 AIR 149
113. AIR 1998 SC 568

19(6) of the Constitution. The reasonable limits that are deemed to be in the public interest can be placed on fundamental rights, including the right to practice a profession or conduct business. This provision enables the prevention of hazardous activities that could harm the environment.

D) Environmental Remedies through Writs

In the ***Dehradun Quarrying Case, AIR 1985[114]***, the installation of safeguards at a chlorine facility in Delhi in the case of *(**M.C. Mehta v Union of India, AIR 1988 SC 1037)**, and other prominent environmental cases were resolved by the Hon'ble Apex Court of India. The Hon'ble Supreme Court of India stated in the ***Vellore Citizens Welfare Forum v. Union of India (1996)*** 5 SCC 647 that *"**the Precautionary Principle"*** and *"**the Polluter Pays Principle"*** are the care and very fundamental components of the *"**Sustainable Development."*** The doctrine of sustainable development is using the resources in the manner that it remains usable even by future generation. It is fundamental principle for environment protection and preservation. The Apex Court of India and several High Courts have exercised their powers laid by the Constitution of India under Article – 32 and Article - 226 of issuing Writ of Mandamus for the protection and preservation of Natural Wildlife and the Environment.

The constitution has given Panchayats the authority to perform actions like forestry, environmental preservation, water management, soil conservation, and promoting ecological aspects at the local and village levels.

In this portion, we will observe the growth of the Laws of Environment in India. The way domestic laws of the land and the Higher Courts of India have shaped laws pertaining to the Environment. The Development of Environmental Laws in India demonstrates how the judicial system, the executive branch, and the legislature work together to create environmental laws in India. As a result, numerous environmental institutions and entities with a variety of functions have been developed.

In India, Concerning various legal frameworks, certain laws are specifically dedicated to the environment and are known as environmental laws. These

---

114. AIR 1985 SC 652

frameworks establish rules and regulations aimed at restricting, safeguarding, and promoting the well-being of the surroundings, including natural resources, ensuring their consumption in a limited and equitable manner. In India, numerous legislations address various aspects of the environment, particularly stemming from the country's active participation in the Stockholm Conference in 1972. This conference marked the first global gathering addressing environmental issues as a paramount concern. Following Mrs. Indira Gandhi's involvement in the conference[115], Indian legislatures took proactive measures to enact laws aimed at protecting the environment from harm and pollution. The primary focus of these laws extended to addressing climate change and overall environmental degradation.

II. Legal Framework for Environmental Protection

i. Environment and Indian Penal Code of 1860

The Indian Penal Code of 1860 is one of the earliest laws enacted by the British Government for India, drafted by the First Law Commission, chaired by Thomas Babington Macaulay has very limited but few provision scope to deal with environmental issues on a micro level. The Pre Independence Laws are applicable in India by the effect of Article – 372(1)[116] of The Indian Constitution. The beginning of Legislation affecting the environment was marked by (IPC) The Indian Penal Code of 1860. The IPC addresses offences involving public health and safety under Chapter XIV. At first, the Section – 268 designates environmental offences as *public nuisances*, and Section 290 punishes the offence by imposing a fine of maximum up to Rs 200/-. Therefore, those who act or fail to act in a way that causes harm to others through environmental contamination may be prosecuted under IPC. Similar to the ruling in the case of ***K. Ramakrishnan v. the State of Kerala (1999)[117]***, was determined that smoking in public places causes public disturbance and is

---

115. Cambridge University Press 978-1-108-49049-8 — Development of Environmental Laws in India
116. The Constitution of India. (1950). Article 372(1).
117. AIR 1999 Ker 385

thus making it illegal under IPC. The Supreme Court again ruled in ***Murli S. Deora v. Union of India (2001)***[118] that smoking in public places violates those who choose not to smoke's fundamental right under Article 21. Smoking not only affects those who are smoking, it affects peoples around smokers and also to the environment at large. Smokers could be classified as those who smoke (active smokers) and those who do not smoke but indirectly inhale cigarette smoke (passive smokers), the active smokers knowingly and deliberately put them in peril but those who do not smoke age gettingaffected adversely even without their knowledge.

Water pollution is prohibited by Section 277, which carries a penalty of up to maximum of 3 (Three) Months in Prison, a fine of up to Rs. 500, or both.[119] The phrase "public spring" or "reservoir" is used in the clause, but the courts have given it a very narrow construction that excludes running/flowing water from rivers, streams, and canals. Similar to this, Section - 278[120] imposes a fine of maximum up to Rs 500/- on one who deliberately and voluntarily degrades the environment by making it unhealthy in a home use, while conducting business in the neighbour, or while passing by on a public pathway. In addition to this, Indian Penal Code, *Sections 426, 430, 431, and 432* punish any pollution caused on by mischief.

In independent India, the fight against pollution in legislation persisted. There are now numerous pieces of legislation in India aimed at preventing pollution and preserving the natural balance. One significant law for environmental protection is ***The Environment (Protection) Act of 1986.***

III. Environment and the Criminal Procedure Code of India

In India, pollution cases are often divided into five basic categories. Tortious liability, nuisance, trespass, negligence, and strict liability are some of these. The Criminal Process Code addresses Public Nuisance in Chapter X. The Criminal Process Code of 1973's Chapter X, i.e. Sections 133 to 143, provide

---

118. (2001) 8 SCC 765.

119. Indian Penal Code, 1860, No. 45 of 1860. (1860)

120. Indian Penal Code, 1860, No. 45 of 1860

effective, prompt, and preventative remedies to deal with public nuisance cases such as unsanitary conditions and contamination of the water, air, and sound.

According to *Section - 133 of the Code of Criminal Procedure, 1973* a District Magistrate (DM) also known as (DC) District Collector or Sub-Divisional Magistrate, (SDM) or any other Executive Magistrate, i.e. ADM Additional District Magistrate, specifically authorized by the Legislature of State on this behest, could issue a conditional order to stop such nuisance, but if the nuisance creator objects or disrupts the exercise, the order will be decided to make absolute. Any order issued in compliance with this paragraph may not be contestedin any civil court. The District Magistrate and District Collector is the same person, the only difference is nature of duty being performed, when the person seating on the chair performs magisterial function, same person is District Magistrate and when the person performs revenue function is District Collector. The power conferred under Section – 133 of CrPc, 1973 is magisterial function.

- **Objective Behind Section: 133 of Code of Criminal Procedure, 1973:**

  Intent or objective of the Section - 133 of Criminal Procedure Code, 1973 is primarily avoiding the annoyance and involves a sense of prompt action coupled with urgency to act, in the notion that if the Executive Magistrate, who has been conferred with the power by the state legislature, does not act swiftly, irrevocable damage would be done to society. A brief analysis of Section 133 of the Criminal Procedure Code, 1973[121] indicates that the language is intended to protect the general public from inconvenience.

  A provision granting the Magistrate broad powers should be exercised with caution and in such a way that they do not become a problem to society. Section 133's goal is to allow the Magistrate to issue swift instructions and act promptly.

---

121. Section 133 of CrPC,1973- Conditional Order for Removal of Nuisance

A Magistrate may initiate Criminal Proceedings against nuisance creator to remove public nuisance under the Criminal Procedure Code of 1973. The Magistrate is required under the Section - 133 of the Cr.P.C. to act swiftly and promptly on information gathered and material received for consideration from a courts document or any reference, including a citizen's complaint pertaining to citizens' grievance.

In the landmark care of Kerala High Court in **K. Ramachandra Mayya v. District Magistrate (1985)**[122] the Hon'ble Kerala High Court affirmed the Magistrate decision to close a stone quarry. The Magistrate addressed local householders' concerns that the quarry's rock blasting caused injury from flying crushed stone was valid in law.

Section- 133 of the Code of Criminal Procedure (Cr.P.C) 1973 was taken in consideration by the Hon'ble Supreme Court of India in the case of **Gobind Singh v. Shanti Sarup, (1978)**[123] where a vent for the defendant's enterprise by an oven bakes caused disturbance, The Court observed:

"We believe that in a case like this when it is not only a particular individual's right at stake, but the welfare, protection, and comfort of the general public, the better approach is to adopt the learned Magistrate's perspective, who observed for himself the threat caused by the bakery'

In the **Municipal Corporation, Ratlam vs. Sh. Vardhichandra and Others (1980)**[124] India's top judicial authority issued a remarkable verdict. The Supreme Court was approached to construe Section - 133 of the Code of Criminal Procedure in this case. The Court in this case observed that the Section - 133 of the Criminal Procedure Code, 1973 are very broad, yet it appears to be as per discretion. When facts for its application are available, judicial

---

122. 1985 (2) KAR LJ

123. 1979 AIR 143

124. 1980 AIR 1622

leniency has an essential impact. As a result, when the Sub-Divisional Magistrate (SDM) has evidence and facts revealing the presence of a nuisance of Public Nature, on him and, is based on materials placed, he considers that certain illegal obstruction, blockage or nuisance should be removed from any public area that is legally in use by the public, he shall respond. So, after going through the process, his judicial authority will be directed towards the obstacle or annoyance caused by the conditions.

As per Section 133 of the Code of Criminal Procedure, 1973 (Cr.P.C), it is the responsibility of the Magistrate to promptly order the cessation of any disturbance within the specified time frame mentioned in the order. This duty is a public obligation derived from public power and performed as part of public activity. Non-compliance with the Magistrate's instructions and order can result in penalties specified in Section 188 of the Indian Penal Code, 1860.

Therefore, any Municipal Officer or Authority who receives an order under Section 133[125] of the Code must comply with it. Disobedience can result in fines or imprisonment if it causes disruption, discomfort, or harm to any person legitimately pursuing their business. The offense is further aggravated if the disobedience poses a risk to human health or safety. When the urgent and mandatory tone of Section 133 of the Criminal Procedure Code, 1973 is combined with the disciplinary tone of Section 188 of the Indian Penal Code, 1860, the prohibition act becomes a mandatory requirement.

The ***Ratlam vs Sh. Vardhichandra and Others***[126] was a breakthrough point in Indian environmental law. The ruling, in this case, has shifted the environmental movement's focus and gained momentum. The Supreme Court recognized municipal governments' duty for environmental preservation in this judgment and included the statute

---

125   Code of Criminal Procedure, 1973, No. 2 of 1974. (1973)

126. AIR 1980 SUPREME COURT 162

of the public nuisance in the Cr.P.C, as an appropriate tool for carrying out such responsibilities.

The landmark ***Govind Singh v. Shanti Sarup (1978)***[127] was the first case law that essentially defined nuisance (1979). Under this provision, the court imposes a conditional order for the removal of the nuisance, which comprises exceedingly wide phrases such as the growth of structures, the discharge of materials, the conduct of commerce, and occupancy.

When the urgent tone of Section - 133 of the Cr.P.C is joined with the harsh and punitive language of Section 188 IPC, the prohibitory act becomes a needed regulation (Ratlam case). This plainly shows that a person may always rely on Section 133 Code of Criminal Procedure to get rid of pollution nuisance.

IV. Environment Specific Laws

Despite several attempts to integrate sustainability into environmental law, the growingeconomy of India has been unable to address environmental concerns, much like any other economy in the world. Furthermore, the economic regulators of India are working to update their country's environmental laws and regulations, which could result in stricter business restrictions and negatively affect the ease of doing business. However, if India and its people do not prioritize these programs, they are unlikely to succeed. As such, it is crucial for the public to cooperate in addressing these concerns since public knowledge is critical to the creation of effective policies. NGOs, non-state actors, and the government should work together to address environmental challenges, and environmental legislation should be enforced more strictly through executive action.

Environmental laws and regulations are a body of rules and regulations that deal with issues such as air quality, water quality, endangered species, and various other aspects of the environment. These laws collectively aim to control human interactions with nature to reduce environmental threats and

---

127. 1979 AIR 143

positively impact public health. Environmental legislative pieces encompass a wide range of laws and regulations, as environmental law must encompass everything around us, including the air we breathe, the natural resources we depend on, the resources we have created for our coexistence, and the flora, fauna, and other creatures that coexist with us on this planet.

India is one of the nations most impacted by climate change, to provide one example. The Indian Economy is dependent on agriculture, the agriculture in India is on the mercy of climate and whether. The good and timely rain yield good produce and untimely rain harms the crop resulting poor agricultural performance.

India's rich cultural heritage has always emphasized the importance of protecting the environment and natural resources. However, the country is currently facing a multitude of environmental challenges that require urgent attention. The impact of climate change on India is particularly concerning, given the vulnerability of several industries and the increased risk of natural disasters like droughts and floods. India's significant contribution to greenhouse gas emissions makes it imperative that the country takes urgent steps to mitigate its environmental impact.

The rivers in India have been revered for centuries, and their importance is deeply ingrained in Indian culture and spirituality. However, increased pollution from residential, industrial, and agricultural sources has put the health of these water bodies in jeopardy, posing a threat to human life on earth. The global impact of environmental degradation cannot be overlooked, and it is essential for countries to work together to safeguard the environment and natural resources[128].

India has taken significant steps to address its environmental challenges, including implementing legislation to enhance energy efficiency, promote clean energy, and prepare for the effects of climate change. However, more needs to be done to ensure a sustainable future for the country and the world. It is crucial for individuals, NGOs, government bodies, and other stakeholders

---

128. ENVIRONMENT AND EARLY SOCIETIES II – RIVER VALLEY CIVILIZATIONS

to work together to create policies that promote sustainable development and protect the environment for future generations.

As a result, initiatives have been taken to raise awareness pertaining to environmental problems among the general public. One to the mode to further increase awareness is Education. Education increases awareness on environmental issues and the environment. It is inner conscience in regards to importance of clean and healthy environment which helps the most in protection of environment. The Governmental Policies, Executive Rules, Judicial Precedents, Regulations Judicial decisions, along with all other set of measures, are mere documents, if are not complied with and if not complied then not enforced. These documents if not successful to bring legislative intent in action in respect of any organizations or individuals just make up a piece of sizable paper work resultant of complex machinery. The question of how much resource, financial and human, India should commit to this regulatory and control work naturally emerges given that the current laws appear not to be very effective in solving the issue and along with stringent additional legislation, strengthening existing legislations is also required.

Need for Environmental Legislations: Environmental concerns are the origin of many national laws. The ecosystem needs to be protected by appropriate legislation; otherwise, the expanding population would wreak havoc on the ecology. The way these rules are enforced is another crucial factor. To prevent additional environmental degradation and pollution, we must forcefully and efficiently enforce the law. Leaving International Political Boundaries and Judicial Authority, pollution is still a significant factor. Environmental concerns are therefore global. Environmental legislation and conventions must be passed and adopted both at the domestic and global levels to avert such issues. While the modern world is becoming more and more concerned with environmental issues on a global scale, pollution problems in developing nations are likewise complex, serious, and expanding quickly. Foreign businesses operating with very less regards for the impact on the domestic and regional environment worsen the already dreadful combination of industrialization with infra development and mass consumerism trends. As pollution can ruin families and communities, it is a larger social issue than merely a health concern. Environmental concerns are intimately linked to how developing nations develop. Nonetheless, a large number of developing nations lack the necessary and enforcement mechanisms or do not have any policies in place to manage pollution[129]

Strong economic growth, enormous urban growth, and quick industrial development— particularly in the petrochemical and heavy industries—have all contributed to a significant rise in pollution emissions. Because effective regulations and laws are necessary to protect the environment, environmental legislation is crucial. People may prevent environmental destruction and preserve it for future generations by increasing environmental consciousness and encouraging environmental education. The law, on the other hand, makes sure that environmental protection is practised in daily life. Businesses, enterprises, the general public, industries, etc. are required by law to preserve the environment and stop environmental deterioration. It imposes harsh punishments on individuals who break the laws and regulations. In the end, this kind of enforcement makes sure that concepts strategies are translated into actionable initiatives to save environment. Some international environmental conventions made an effort to solve global environmental challenges. The UN (United Nations) started putting more and more efforts on environmental concerns, after the Stockholm Conference in the year (1972). Seventy international treaties, declarations, charters, accords, and other documents have since been ratified by several countries. These attempts were made to protect the environment and strike a systematic balance in environmental protection and preservation and human along with infrastructural development activities.

The majority of our environmental legislation was passed by state or federal legislatures. Generally speaking, these Acts grant regulators the authority to create regulations to carry them out.

---

129. 79 Towards a Second Generation in Environmental Laws in the Asian and Pacific Region- Edited by – Lye Lin- Heng with Maria Socorro Z. Manguiat, IUCN International Law Programme

i. The Public Liability Insurance Act and Rules 1991 and Amendment, 1992

The Public Liability Insurance Act, 1991 and Rules, of 1991 and Amendment Act of, 1992 have been introduced to give individuals, Public Liability Insurance if they are accidentally injured when handling any substance which is hazardous[130]

Public Liability Act, of 1991 regulates Mandatory Liability Insurance. Companies have to maintain standards in respect of hazardous substance. The aggrieved who have been injured can claim from the negligent owner, if the negligence is proved on the part the claim would be successful.

The Public Liability Insurance Act of 1991 in India provides for the payment of compensation to victims in case of any damage caused by handling hazardous substances. It mandates that any person handling hazardous substances has to take out an insurance policy covering liability for any damage that may be caused to third parties due to handling of such hazardous substances. The insurance policy covers the owner of the hazardous substance in case of any damage caused to people, property, or the environment due to an accident. The compensation to the victims of the accident is paid from this insurance coverage, and it relieves the owner of the hazardous substance from the burden of paying a huge amount of compensation from their own pocket.

The purpose of this act is to ensure that in case of any accident involving hazardous substances, the victims and affected persons are provided with immediate relief and compensation. The act helps in preventing any negligence or carelessness on the part of the owners handling hazardous substances, as they have to take out insurance to cover for any possible damages. It also helps in creating awareness among the owners about the risks involved in handling hazardous substances and promotes responsible behavior towards the environment and the society.

---

130. Public Liability Insurance Act 1991, Ministry of Environment, Forest and Climate Change

In summary, the Public Liability Insurance Act of 1991 is an important legislation in India that ensures that the victims of accidents caused by hazardous substances are promptly compensated. It encourages the owners handling hazardous substances to be cautious and responsible, as they have to take out insurance to cover for any possible damages caused by their activities.

ii. The National Environmental Tribunal Act, 1995, Amendment, 2010

The Act intends to compensate for harm caused to people at large, properties, and environment pertaining to hazardous substance-related operations. The three key objectives are:

Handling cases associated with preservation and environment protection, the forestspreservation, and protection of other natural resources quickly and effectively, in fastrack manner and specialized mechanism. The Tribunal is also hearing every case that has previously been on hold.

- To uphold environmental legal rights.

- It also takes into account allowing relief and recompense to those, harmed by the damage.

The following are the key elements of the Amendment:

- Every Indian citizen now has the equal opportunity to apply to the NGT,

- Ensure that when considering appeals and issuing rulings, courts consider the precautionary principle; the polluter pays principle, intergenerational equity, and the sustainable development principle.

The primary location for setting up tribunals in New Delhi. The four main locations for holding tribunals are regarded to be Bhopal, Kolkata, Pune, and Kolkata. To encourage environmental conservation and to preserve sections of the environment, such as forests and other national resources, the tribunals were established to offer an efficient and quick solution. Also, it offers relief through restitution and encourages the protection of the afflicted person. The tribunal contains at least 10 judges and more experts under the direction of a chairperson who sits on the primary bench.

iii. The National Environment Appellate Authority Act, 1997

The Act of 1997 was passed to deal with appeals concerning limitations on regions where certain sectors, company categories, and so on are needed to conform to defined protections. The National Environment Appellate Authority Act entered into force on January 30, 1997. With the increase in pollution and the environmental damage increased with the time in India due to several catastrophes, the Apex Court of India and the Government of India accepted the need for the establishment of specialized environmental courts to examine cases involvingecological problems as well as the harm carried out to the environment. A law was passed to create the National Environment Appellate Authority, which will hear appeals about area restrictions, deal with topics covered by The Act of 1986, and handle matters related thereto.

The National Environment Appellate Authority Act was enacted by the Union Government to create the National Environment Appellate Authority. This body is responsible for carrying out various functions as described in the Act, which has 23 sections. The Authority is made up of a Chairperson, a Vice-Chairperson, and three other members who are all appointed by the President and are considered public servants. The head office of the Authority is located in Delhi, and its members hold office for a term of 3 years, with the possibility of reappointment. The President can remove any member from office if they are found to have engaged in misconduct.

As per the provisions outlined in the previously mentioned Act, individuals who are not content with environmental clearance orders pertaining to specific areas have the opportunity to appeal to the Appellate Authority. The Authority is required to settle such appeals within a 90-day timeframe and possesses the authority to call upon witnesses, document statements, and oversee its procedures in a way comparable to that of a civil court. The Chairman of the Appellate Authority is responsible for performing financial and administrative duties, while all other members must comply with the Chairperson's orders as outlined in Section 13 of the Act.

According to the National Environment Appellate Authority Act, the Appellate Authority has sole jurisdiction over the matters for which it has been established, and no other civil or other authority is authorized to hear appeals related to those matters. The procedures conducted before the Appellate Authority is regarded as judicial proceedings, as per the definition provided in Sections 193, 219, and 228 of the Indian Criminal Code, under Section 16 of the Act.

Legal action against the Union Government is not permissible, as the Act and the establishment of the Appellate Authority were executed in good faith to benefit the public. Those who oppose environmental protection are subject to the orders of the Appellate Authority, which was established in accordance with the Act. Failure to comply with these orders may result in imprisonment for up to seven years or a fine of up to 1 Lakh rupees, or both, as per Sections 17 and 18 of the Act.

The Union Government is authorized under sections - 21 and 22 of the Act to enact regulations and address matters related to the compensation and benefits of the Appellate Authority's members, as well as the financial and executive powers of the Chairperson, as specified in Sec - 13 of the Act.

Starting from January 1, 1998, the Biomedical Waste, 1998 came into force. These regulations were issued by the Central Government to handle and manage biomedical waste produced by hospitals, clinics, and other institutions. The purpose of these regulations was to ensure the appropriate scientific management of bio waste, as authorized by sections 6, 8, and 25 of the EP Act, 1986.

iv. The Biomedical Waste (Management and Handling) Rules, 1998

The term "biomedical waste" refers to any waste produced during the diagnosis, treatment, or immunization of humans or animals, as well as during related research activities, and the production or testing of biological substances, including the categories specified in the Regulations. The Biomedical Waste

(Management and Handling) Rules, 1998 aim to simplify the disposal, collection, and classification of hospital waste.[131]

All entities that generate biomedical waste, such as hospitals, nursing homes, clinics, dispensaries, veterinary facilities, animal houses, pathological laboratories, or blood banks,are required by law to take appropriate measures to handle the waste in a manner that safeguards public health and the environment.

To achieve the goal of the said Act, the following rules must be followed for in regards to biomedical waste:

1. Such waste cannot be mixed with any other types of garbage.

2. Such waste must be separated in container or bag at the place of generation, before being stored, transported, treated, and disposed of. The labels for the containers must follow Schedule III.

Each occupier of an institution who produces, collects, receives, stores, transports, treats, and/or handles biomedical waste must apply for authorization from the Board using Form 1.

The State Pollution Control Board has is Prescribed Authority for granting authorizations. Board will only issue authorizations after being satisfied with the conditions and requirements. Every occupier/operator is required by law to submit an annual report in Form II by the deadline of January 31 of each year, which must include details about the types and quantities of medical waste handled during the previous years. At the end of March each year, the required authority must provide this information to the CPCB.

In case of an accident at a facility or during the transportation of biomedical waste, the authorized person must report the incident immediately to the designated authority by submitting Form III.

If someone disagrees with an order issued by the authority designated under the Biomedical Waste Management and Handling Rules, they can appeal to the appropriate state or union territory authority within 30 days of

---

131. The Biomedical Waste (Management and Handling) Rules, 1998

the order being notified. However, if the appellant has a valid reason for not filing the appeal within the stipulated time, the authority may still consider it even after the deadline.

The State Pollution Control Board (SPCB) has the power, under the Environment Protection Act, to take legal action against individuals or entities that violate the rules for managing biomedical waste. Such violations can result in imprisonment to 5 years and a monitory fine. Furthermore, the Board can also use its authority, granted by the Central Government, to order the closure of hospitals, clinics, or institutions that do not comply with Sec - 5 of the Environment Protection Act, 1986.

v. The Environment (Sitting for Industrial Projects) Rules, 1999

The Environment Rules, 1999 outline regulations concerning selection of appropriate sites for industrial projects, including the identification of areas that should be avoided, the necessary precautions be taken while choosing a site, and the protection measures that must be taken into consideration.

vi. The Municipal Solid Wastes (Management and Handling) Rules, 2000

Each local authority is subject to these Rules. They are responsible for ensuring that the separation, storage, transportation, processing, and disposal of solid waste created by municipality are done so in conformity with the applicable laws and regulations. The municipal authorities, who are in charge of managing municipal solid trash, are putting into effect The Regulations, of 2000. (MSW). The Regulations came into effect in September 2000 and stipulate that the management of solid waste produced in cities must adhere to the requirements for collection, segregation, storage, transportation, processing, and disposal set forth in the Rules. During the reporting year, the Central Pollution Control Board (CPCB) reached out to State Pollution Control Boards (SPCBs) and Pollution Control Committees (PCCs) in union territories, who provided feedback on various aspects of the Regulation. SPCBs and PCCs persuaded local authorities to seek approvals and develop solid waste management plans.

vii. The Batteries (Management and Handling) Rules, 2001

The Batteries Rules of 2001 were established in India to govern the management and handling of used lead-acid batteries. The goal was to prevent improper disposal, which can cause environmental pollution and health risks. These regulations apply to all parties involved in the manufacturing, processing, sale, purchase, and use of lead-acid batteries, as well as those who participate in their collection, storage, transport, and recycling. The guidelines prescribe procedures for collecting, storing, transporting, and recycling used batteries. They also require battery recyclers to obtain registration and authorization. Battery manufacturers and recyclers are expected to create systems for collecting used batteries, ensure environmentally responsible recycling, and maintain records of their operations.

All entities involved in battery management and handling, such as Manufacturers, Suppliers, Assemblers, Importers, Auctioneers, Bulk Consumers, and Consumers, are subject to the regulations set out in the Batteries Rules of 2001. These guidelines outline procedures for the collection, storage, transportation, and recycling of used lead-acid batteries, with the objective of preventing environmental pollution and promoting sustainable development.

The followings are the manufacturer's and importers' legal obligations:

➢ Ensuring the collection of used batteries by the Schedule of new battery sales, This phrase means that the obligation to collect used batteries does not apply to original equipment manufacturers and bulk consumers.

➢ This means that manufacturers and importers must ensure used batteries they collect are of the same type and character as the newly sold batteries. In other words, they should not collect batteries that are different from the ones they sell.

➢ To submit a Form-I half-yearly report on their sales and buybacks to the State Board no later than June 30 and December 31 of each year;

> ➢ To establish collection points—individually or collectively—in various locations to receive used batteries from customers or dealers;

> ➢ To make sure that the used batteries are exclusively transported to the designated recyclers;

> ➢ To see to it that the appropriate preparations with dealers are completed for secure transportation to the locations of registered recyclers;

> ➢ To prevent environmental harm from occurring while being transported;

> ➢ To This means that manufacturers and importers must educate the general public about the risks associated with lead, the importance of returning used batteries to authorized dealers or collection facilities. In other words, they should raise awareness among the public about the proper disposal of used batteries and the potential harm that can result from improper disposal.

> ➢ To apply the global recycling symbol on batteries;

> ➢ To only purchase the recycled lead from authorized recyclers;

> ➢ To bring any violation committed by the dealers to State Boards or the Ministry of Environment and Forests' attention;

> ➢ To guarantee that only authorized dealers will be sold new batteries.

viii. The Noise Pollution (Regulation and Control) (Amendment) Rules, 2010

The Noise Pollution Regulations, 2000[1] aim to regulate and control sources of noise to ensure that ambient air quality requirements related to noise are met. The primary objective is to reduce noise pollution, and these regulations establish guidelines for achieving this goal. While the use of loudspeakers or public address systems is permitted during night-time cultural or religious events between 10:00 p.m. and midnight, their use is prohibited at night, except in enclosed spaces such as auditoriums, conference rooms, community halls, or banquet halls. Those using loudspeakers or public address systems must maintain noise levels within 10 dB (A) above the ambient noise regulations of the specified area or 75 dB (A), whichever is lower.

Owners of private sound systems or other sound-producing equipment are not allowed to violate the noise limits set for the location where they are utilized by more than 5 dB (A).

It is forbidden to set off sound-emitting fireworks at night or in quiet areas. The Amendment's main characteristics are as follows:

The use of loudspeakers, sound systems, or amplifiers is prohibited at night; exception is enclosed areas such as auditoriums, meeting rooms, banquet halls, and during public contingencies. If loudspeakers are used, the noise level must not exceed Ten decibels (dB) or Seventy Five decibels (dB), whichever is lower. Horns should only be used in residential areas in case of an emergency. Additionally, construction machinery that creates noise should not be used after dark.

Using sound amplifiers or playing any music, or trumpet or beats or sounds instrument, or a horn that blows either melody or pressure or playing a musical performance or another type of entertainment to draw crowds or sound of firecrackers bursting or utilizing a public address system or a loudspeaker, are prohibited in the silent zone.

Individuals who violate the rules or provisions outlined in this Act may be subject to penalties, including imprisonment for a maximum of 5 years, a fine of up to 1 Lakh rupees, or both. In the event of ongoing failure or violation, an additional fine of up to 5,000 rupees may be imposed for each subsequent day that the violation continues. The perpetrator shall be punished with imprisonment for a term that may extend to 7 years if the violation persists for more than a year following the date of conviction.

ix. The Air (Prevention and Control of Pollution) Act, 1981

The Air Act, 1981 aims to prevent, control, and abate air pollution in India. It provides a legalframework for the central and state governments to take action against air pollution and establish regulatory bodies to carry out the provisions of the act. The act also empowers the regulatory bodies to impose penalties on industries and individuals who violate its provisions[55].

The Air (Prevention and Control of Pollution) Act, 1981 has played an important role in improving the air quality in India by requiring industries and factories to install pollution control equipment and regulating emissions from vehicles. However, air pollution remains a major problem in many parts of the country and continued efforts are needed to effectively address the issue. The central and state governments, along with the public and private sectors, need to work together to implement and enforce the provisions of the act and other measures to prevent and control air pollution.

The Air (Prevention and Control of Pollution) Act, 1981 aims to prevent and control air pollution in India, and the Central Pollution Control Board (CPCB) and State Pollution Control Board (SPCB) are responsible for implementing and enforcing the provisions of the act. The act requires industries and factories to install pollution control equipment and regulates emissions from vehicles and the use of certain fuels that contribute to air pollution. Despite these efforts, air pollution remains a significant issue in many parts of the country, particularly in urban areas like New Delhi. The WHO has identified New Delhi as one of the most polluted cities in the world, with high levels of particulate matter and other pollutants contributing to respiratory diseases and other health problems.

> An officer with CPCB authorization

> A person who has filed a grievance with the board or a board-authorized officer.

As per the legislation, the State Board must be consulted by the State Government before designating an air pollution area in a particular region of the State. Additionally, the State Government may create a new pollution area or a portion thereof by combining, reducing, or merging one or more existing air pollution zones.

The Air (Prevention and Control of Pollution) Act, 1981 empowers state governments to take measures to prevent and control air pollution, which includes issuing notices in the Official Gazette to prohibit the use of any fuel or equipment that may contribute to air pollution after consulting with the State Pollution Control Board. The state governments can also prohibit the burning of any substance that causes or is likely to cause air pollution, including non-fuel materials. This is an important measure to help reduce air pollution and improve the air quality in the affected areas.

x. Scheduled Tribes and Other Traditional Forest Dwellers (Recognition ofForest Rights) Act, 2006 (FRA)

The Scheduled Tribes and Other Traditional Forest Dwellers Act, 2006 was enacted by the Indian Parliament to recognize and vest forest rights and occupation in forest land in forest- dwelling Scheduled Tribes and other traditional forest dwellers who have been residing in such forests for generations. The act was passed to correct the historical injustice done to these forest-dwelling communities and to ensure their livelihoods and rights to forest resources are protected. The act provides for the recognition and vesting of forest rights, including the right to ownership, access to collect, use and dispose of minor forest produce, grazing rights, and other community rights such as the right to protect, regenerate, and conserve forests and wildlife. The act also establishes the process for the identification and verification of forest-dwelling communities and their rights, and for the settlement of disputes related to forest rights.

The Scheduled Tribes and Other Traditional Forest Dwellers Act, 2006 was enacted by the Indian Parliament to recognize and vest forest rights and occupation in forest land in forest- dwelling Scheduled Tribes and other traditional forest dwellers who have been residing in such forests for generations. The act was passed to correct the historical injustice done to these forest-dwelling communities and to ensure their livelihoods and rights to forest resources are protected. The act provides for the recognition and vesting of forest rights, including the right to ownership, access to collect, use and dispose of minor forest produce, grazing rights, and other community rights such as the right to protect, regenerate, and conserve forests and wildlife. The act also establishes the process for the identification and verification of forest-dwelling communities and their rights, and for the settlement of disputes related to forest rights.

The main objective of act is to empower forest-dwelling communities by giving them legal rights over forest resources and to protect their traditional and customary rights. The act recognizes and vests forest rights, including individual and community rights, in forest land for habitation, cultivation, grazing, and other traditional uses .The act provides setting up of Forest Rights Committees at the village level to facilitate the recognition and vesting of forest rights. The committees are responsible for preparing and submitting claims to the Sub-Divisional Level Committee (SDLC) for approval.

The FRA has been hailed as landmark legislation for its potential to address historical injustices and protect the rights of forest-dwelling communities. However, its implementation has been uneven and has faced challenges, including lack of awareness among forest- dwelling communities, inadequate resources for implementation, and opposition from forest department officials and other stakeholders.

The Act acknowledges and awards occupancy rights and forest rights to other traditional forest dwellers (OTFDs) and (FDSTs) who lived in these forests for many generations. The Department of Tribal Affairs serves as the Act's chair. The law also establishes duties and authority for the conservation of biodiversity, responsible FDST and OTFD use, and upkeep of ecological balance. In ensuring FDST and OTFD livelihoods and food security, it promotes forest protection mechanisms. For the survival and viability of forest ecosystems, it seeks to redress the colonial injustice of the FDST and OTFD. The law distinguishes four categories of rights.

> **Title rights:** Up to a maximum area of Four hectares, it grants the FDST and OTFD the right to possess land farmed by tribes or inhabited by forest dwellers. Ownership does not extend to additional land; rather, it only pertains to the property that the relevant family has been cultivating.

> **Right to use:** Dweller rights include the right to use pastures, pasture trails, and other smaller forest products.

> **Right to Manage:** The right to manage all communal forest resources, including the ability to regenerate, conserves, and uses them sustainably, falls under the category of forest management rights.

> **Relief and development rights:** Rehabilitating people who have been forcibly relocated or evicted, as well as providing them with necessities, is subject to constraints for forest conservation.

Objective

> To correct the historical wrongs committed against the populations that live in the forests.

> To make the system of forest conservation stronger by including the responsibilities and power of forest rights holders for ecological balance, biodiversity preservation, and sustainable usage.

> The legislation also contains requirements to guarantee sustainable usage, biodiversity preservation, and upkeep of ecological harmony by owners of forest rights.

> To ensure land tenure, livelihood, and food security of the scheduled tribes and other traditional forest dwellers.

Thus, the Act gives forest dwellers the authority to use forest resources in the same way they have in the past, to protect, conserve, and manage forests, to shield forest dwellers from forcible evictions, and to also provide for basic infrastructure and development needs for the community of forest dwellers.

xi. The Forest (Conservation) Act, 1980

The Forest Act, 1980 has been amended several times since its enactment, with the most recent amendment in 2017. The amendments have aimed to strengthen the act's provisions for conservation and management of forests, enhance the role of local communities and gram sabhas (village councils) in decision-making regarding forest land, and streamline the process of compensatory afforestation. The act also provides for the establishment of a

National Committee for Conservation of Forests and Wildlife to advise the central government on issues related to forest conservation and management. The Forest (Conservation) Act, 1980 is an important law that has helped to conserve India's forests and protect its wildlife[132].

Under the act, state governments are required to submit proposals for diversion of forest land to the central government for approval. The central government considers the proposals and grants approval if it is satisfied that the diversion is necessary and unavoidable, and that adequate compensatory forestation measures will be taken.

The Forest (Conservation) Act, 1980 has faced challenges in its implementation. The inadequate compensation for forest dwellers and tribal communities who are affected by the diversion of forest land has been a major issue. The act mandates that the affected people must be compensated for the loss of their forest land, but in practice, the compensation has been inadequate, leading to conflicts between forest dwellers and government authorities.

Additionally, weak enforcement of the compensatory forestation provisions has also been a challenge. The act requires that any diversion of forest land for non-forestry purposes must be accompanied by compensatory forestation measures, but in practice, these measures have not been implemented effectively. As a result, the ecological balance has been disturbed, leading to further degradation of forests and loss of biodiversity.

To address these challenges, the government has taken several measures, including increasing compensation for forest dwellers and tribal communities, strengthening the enforcement of compensatory afforestation provisions, and involving local communities in the management of forests. However, more needs to be done to ensure the effective implementation of the act and to promote sustainable forest management in India.

The Forest Rights Act of 2006 was established to protect the rights of forest communities to the land and other resources that are essential to their way of life. The Act not only grants community rights, but also allows forest residents

---

132. The Forest (Conservation) Act, 1980

to consume minor forest products. Furthermore, those who have forest rights must maintain and preserve the animals, biodiversity, and forest resources in the area. As forests are a precious resource, it is important that everyone works to safeguard them. Deforestation disrupts the natural cycles of the environment, so regulations are necessary to protect forests. The main objective of the Act is to conserve forests and the variety of plant and animal life they support, while maintaining the integrity and range of the forests. Additionally, forest areas cannot be used for grazing, agriculture, or commercial purposes.

The Objectives of the Forest Rights Act, 2006

➢ To rectify previous wrongs done to people that live in the forests.

➢ By merging the duties and power of those who have forest rights, the conservation regime of the woods will be strengthened in order to support sustainable use, biodiversity preservation, and ecological balance.

➢ To ensure land tenure, livelihood, and food security of STs and other traditional dwellers.

The Forest Rights Act of 2006 empowers the forest-dwelling communities to protect and conserve the forests and their resources, as well as to participate in the decision-making process that affects them. It also aims to provide social and economic security to the forest dwellers while safeguarding the biodiversity and ecological balance of the forests. Overall, the Act recognizes the traditional rights of forest-dwelling communities and aims to create a balance between conservation and development.

xii. The Wildlife Protection Act, 1972

The Wildlife Protection Act, 1972 is a crucial legislation for the conservation and protection of India's wildlife. It provides for the establishment of protected areas such as national parks, wildlife sanctuaries, and conservation reserves for the conservation of wildlife and their habitats. The act also regulates the hunting and poaching of wild animals and the trade in wildlife and their products. The act has been amended several times to strengthen its provisions and address emerging issues related to wildlife conservation.

The act establishes protected areas such as national parks, wildlife sanctuaries, and conservation reserves for the protection and conservation of wildlife. It also provides for the appointment of wildlife wardens, who are to manage and protection of wildlife in their jurisdiction.

Under the act, killing, or capturing of any wild animal or bird is strictly prohibited except under special circumstances, such as when an animal is declared as a man-eater or a threat to human life. The act also prohibits the trade in wildlife and their products, except for scientific or educational purposes.

The Wildlife Protection Act, 1972 has played a crucial role in the conservation of wildlife in India. However, the implementation of the act has faced several challenges, including the lack of resources and capacity for enforcement, and conflicts between conservation and development interests.

The Wildlife (Protection) Act of 1972 is legislation in India that seeks to protect wild animals and their habitats. It also prohibits the trade in wildlife and wildlife products, and sets penalties for offenses under the Act. The Act has been amended several times to strengthen its provisions, and has played a pivotal role in the conservation of several species of wildlife in India.

The applicable legislation still has significant loopholes, nevertheless. The application of theoretical laws in real life is lacking. Moreover, meddling from the bureaucracy dilutes the intent of the legislation.

Under the 'Wildlife Protection Act, of 1972' Hunting of animals is prohibited. Hunting of wildlife is forbidden as stated in the appendix. There are other exceptions, though. In the sake of protecting itself, another animal, or both, the State authority may order the slaughter or harm of any animal. Every animal that was killed or hurt served a governmental function and was not a crime. The government could consent to the killing of some animals for scientific research.

Objectives of the Wildlife Protection Act, 1972

➤ To protect the environment,

  ➤ Put in practice the decisions made at Stockholm UN Conference on the Environmentin 1972

  ➤ Those endangering environment will be punished.

  ➤ Enforcing environmental laws if they are not already covered by any other enforcedlaw

  ➤ Provide authority to the government to implement strict protection measures forenvironment,

  ➤ Primary goal of the law is to protect animals, birds, and plants,

  ➤ This Act provides for appointment of wildlife wardens and the establishing wildlifeadvisory boards to assist with the implementation of the Act.

Each person who has been granted permission under this Act is entitled to access, inspect, hold, and occupy any building. He can halt both cars and ships and inspect them. He has the right to go into any building for inspection. Also, he has the right to keep any confined animal, including wild animals, domestic animals, animals used as trophies or untreated animals, as well as any particular plant or a section of it.

xiii. The Water (Prevention and Control of Pollution) Act, 1974

The Water Act of 1974 establishes the CPCB and SPCB to prevent, control, and combat water pollution. It mandates the maintenance of water quality and the avoidance of pollution in public water bodies, and prohibits the dumping of waste in such bodies. Additionally, it prescribes limitations for the release of pollutants into water sources and obliges industrial establishments to obtain permission from the appropriate control board before discharging waste. The Act also establishes a system for resolving disputes that arise as a result of its implementation and provides for the inspection of premises and the seizure of polluting materials. The legislation is a critical component of

India's environmental law framework and serves to ensure that the nation's water supply is healthy and secure.[59]

Under the Act, the CPCB and State Pollution Control Boards are responsible for enforcing water quality standards, issuing permits for discharges, and taking action against polluters. The Act also provides for the establishment of pollution control committees at the local level, which are responsible for monitoring water quality and identifying sources of pollution.

One of the key provisions of the Act is the requirement to obtain consent to operate from the control board before commencing operations for industries. The consent sets out the conditions under which the industry can discharge pollutants into water bodies, and failure to comply with these conditions can result in penalties and even closure of the industry. The Act also provides for the check of industries and the power to take samples of effluents for testing.

In addition to regulating industrial discharges, the Act also regulates the disposal of sewage and other waste into water bodies. It requires local authorities to provide adequate sewage treatment facilities and to ensure that untreated sewage is not discharged into water bodies.

Overall, the Water Act plays a crucial role in protecting India's water resources and ensuring that they are safe and healthy for all to use. animal, including wild animals, domestic animals, animals used as trophies or untreated animals, as well as any particular plant or a section of it.

At the Stockholm summit, it was decided to establish uniform regulations throughout the country to address significant environmental challenges that pose a threat to the health of our environment. The Water Act of 1974 is the most important legislative action taken by Parliament in this regard, which is also the first comprehensive law that sets up administrative bodies to prevent water pollution. The Control Board at the Centre and State levels was established under this act to ensure the quality of water and prevent the dumping of household and industrial waste into waterways without proper treatment, resulting from industrialization and urbanization. To address these issues, the CPCB and SPCB were created in the states. This act was enacted to combat and reduce pollution in India, and it focuses on maintaining the integrity of water by establishing Boards and giving them the necessary authority to achieve the Act's objectives. The Water Act of 1974 is accompanied by its corresponding regulations, the Water (Procedure for Exchange of Business) Regulations of 1974.

The Act of 1974 is a comprehensive law with a total of sixty sections for the prevention and management of water pollution, with particular modifications made in 1978. The Act also provides for, among other things, the establishment of Central and State Boards for preventing water contamination, the ability to conduct water tests and their examination, the release of sewage or exchange effluents, requests, updates, the least and most severe punishments, the distribution of wrongdoers' names, violations by Companies and Government divisions, awareness of violations, water research facilities, investigation, and so on.

xiv. The Ozone-Depleting Substances (Regulation and Control) Rules, 2000

The Ozone-Depleting Substances Rules, 2000 is an Indian law that was enacted to regulate the production, use, and disposal of ozone-depleting substances (ODS). These rules were introduced under the Environment Protection Act, 1986, which is the primary legislation governing environmental protection in India[133].

The main objective of the rules is to protect the layer by controlling the, use, and disposal of ODS, which are chemicals that deplete the earth's protective ozone layer. The rules require manufacturers and users of ODS to comply with specific guidelines, standards, and restrictions to minimize the release of ODS into the atmosphere.

Under the rules, the import and export of ODS are prohibited except for specified purposes such as research, critical use exemptions, and essential use exemptions. The rules also prohibit the production and sale of ODS unless a valid license is obtained from the competent authority.

---

133. The Ozone-Depleting Substances (Regulation and Control) Rules, 2000

The Ozone-Depleting Substances Rules, 2000 provide specific deadlines for the elimination of various ozone-depleting substances (ODS) and regulate the production, commercial import, and export of goods containing ODS. With the exception of metered-dose inhalers and other medical applications, these regulations prohibit the use of ODS, such as CFCs, halons, carbon tetrachloride, and methyl chloroform.

xv. Coastal Regulation Zone Notification, 2018

After receiving feedback from various stakeholders including coastal states, UTs, and others, it became clear that a complete revision of the existing notification was necessary. The feedback focused on various aspects such as the preservation of marine and coastal ecosystems, coastal area development, eco-tourism, livelihood opportunities, and sustainable development of coastal communities. To address these concerns, the MoEF established a committee in June 2014[134]. The committee, led by Shailesh Nayank, submitted its recommendations in 2015, which were then reviewed in conjunction with other relevant Indian government ministries and members of parliament from coastal states and union territories.

Under the *Shailesh Nayak Committee's advice,* it was announced. In addition to focusing on natural calamities like the rise in sea level brought on by global warming, this legislation encourages sustainable growth. Also, it safeguards the livelihoods of regional populations, notably fishers, while preserving wildlife.

The government received numerous recommendations and feedback, which highlighted the importance of sustainable development and conservation of the coastal environment. As a result, the government has approved the Coastal Regulation Zone Notification 2018, which is expected to significantly contribute to fulfilling the aspirations of coastal communities while also safeguarding the welfare of marginalized and vulnerable populations.

In addition to fostering economic growth, the proposed CRZ Notification, 2018 would increase activity in the coastal zones while also upholding their conservation principles. It will improve lives and strengthen India's economy

---

134. Coastal Regulation Zone Notification, 2018

in addition to producing a considerable amount of new jobs. The new warning is anticipated to revitalize the coastal regions while lessening their vulnerability.

xvi. The Energy Conservation Act, 2001

The world is full of energy. It flows through our bodies, flies through the air, and the sun bears down on us. It's all over. So what precisely is energy, you ask? How is it preserved, too?

Energy conservation does not imply making the most of a finite resource by consuming it or producing more of it, but rather using the existing energy resources wisely otherwise we are putting ourselves in a position where we will eventually run out of energy. To encourage the limited supply to begin rebuilding itself, conservation involves reducing demand for it. In many circumstances, it is desirable to replace the consumed energy with a different option. To prevent oil and other resources from fully running out, fossil fuels can be conserved by discovering other resources and substituting them. This will hasten the filling of the oil field.

The ratification of the Energy Conservation Act, of 2001 marked a significant development in improving energy efficiency and cutting waste. It deals with requirements for appliances and equipment's energy use. Moreover, it specifically addresses the issue of energy consumption regulations and other requirements for customers. Natural resources in India are being depleted as a result of the country's expanding population and a corresponding rise in energy consumption. Once these resources are gone, they cannot be replenished in the same form. According to the law, customers who utilize less energy than the established norms and criteria will get certificates for their efforts. Customers that use more energy than what is required by the norms and regulations may acquire an energy savings certificate to bring their usage into compliance. According to the Act, new construction must adhere to the Energy Conservation Building Code, big energy consumers must follow energy consumption regulations, and equipment must fulfill energy performance requirements and display energy consumption labels. It proposes building regulations for commercial structures that conserve energy. The Act established the (BEE) as a legislative organization.

Energy conservation requires each individual to develop a habit to save energy, such as turning off the lights when we leave a room or shutting down the computer instead of putting it in sleep mode. The expression is frequently mistaken for "efficient use of energy." It entails using energy-efficient things in daily life and making sure they are in good functioning order. Energy conservation not only keeps the environment greener but also prevents the depletion of energy supplies, lowers the cost of operating equipment, and lengthens the useful lives of those appliances.

The 14th of December is recognized as International Energy Conservation Day. An approach to lower energy demand is energy protection. Monitoring energy is a crucial way to reduce the burden on the environment and lower power prices. Energy conservation promotes an eco-friendly lifestyle by providing energy, which saves money and the environment at the same time.

xvii. The Biological Diversity Act, 2002

The biodiversity loss poses a threat to all living species on Earth and could lead to an imbalance in the ecosystem that could ultimately destroy the natural environment. India is home to a vast array of rare species and is one of the most biologically diverse countries globally. However, various factors such as overpopulation, resource depletion, climate change, habitat loss due to human development, and increasing pollution levels pose a severe threat to India's biodiversity.

India already had several environmental laws in place before the Diversity Act of 2002 was enacted. However, the need for this Act arose due to a gap in existing legislation, which was identified after India ratified the Convention on Biological Diversity in Rio de Janeiro. The Diversity Act of 2002 was introduced to address this gap and provide a framework for sustainable development and conservation of India's natural resources.

The Biological Diversity Act, 2002, has several objectives aimed at conserving biodiversity in India. Section - 36 deals with the preparation of a National Biodiversity Plan and a National Biodiversity Strategy, while Section - 37 deals with the notification of areas of bio importance by the Governments of State. Section - 38 empowers the Central Government to declare species as endangered, critically endangered, or threatened, and prohibit their hunting, killing, capturing, or trade.

The Section 21 of the Act mandates that the (NBA) and (SBBs) should ensure that the benefits arising out of the use of biological resources, their derivatives and knowledge are shared in a fair way with the stakeholders or local communities that have conserved and protected these resources. This provision is meant to ensure that the benefits of biodiversity conservation and sustainable use are shared with the communities that have traditionally used and conserved these resources.

Resources or traditional knowledge are regarded as being freely accessible if they haven't been granted by the state or any other private person or entity through patents or grants. Even with these precautions, losses continue to occur every year. India remains far behind other countries in its efforts to safeguard biodiversity, even though some Act's provisions are progressive. The local community should be made familiar of this Legislation on biodiversity. India's biodiversity has to be well protected by implementing its legal system and regulations. The number of vulnerable and endangered species has increased by 7.8% between 2014 and 2017 and it is a huge debate about whether the said Act has attained and how far has been successful in attaining its goal.

To put the Act into action and achieve the intended objectives, both the government and each individual must make efforts in their ways. The Act may be more effectively implemented if local governments, farmers, and scientific institutions were to form a network and integrate.

xviii. The National Green Tribunal Act, 2010

The Act of 2010 was created to provide legal and administrative solutions for individuals who have been impacted by pollution and other environmental damage. As a result, the (NGT) was formed in the same year. The NGT is a specialized judicial body with expertise in resolving environmental disputes in India. [64]

The NGT is responsible for resolving issues related to environmental preservation, protection of natural resources, and the enforcement of environmental rights. Its decisions are final and enforceable, and it has the power to provide damages and remedies to those who have suffered harm.

The NGT is present in five zones, including North, Central, East, South, and West, with the headquarters located in Delhi. The NGT consists of at least ten and no more than twenty judicial members, a Chairman who sits on the Main Bench, and at least ten and no more than twenty expert members. Any individual who has been affected by environmental harm related to the laws listed in Schedule I of the National Green Tribunal Act, 2010 can approach the Tribunal for compensation and redress.

1.   The Air (Prevention and Control of Pollution) Act, 1981;

2.   The Environment (Protection) Act, 1986;

3.   The Public Liability Insurance Act, 1991;

4.   The Biological Diversity Act, 2002.

Any civil matters containing a significant environmental or related concern fall under the jurisdiction of the Tribunal. Also, under the aforementioned laws, anybody who feels wronged by an order or directive issued by one of the appellate authorities may appeal it to the National Green Tribunal.

The Act does not mandate that parties seeking redressal in engagement a lawyer, as they can approach the Tribunal in person by adhering to the necessary format. The NGT is responsible for resolving cases within 6 months of appointment. The Tribunal's role is essential in addressing significant environmental concerns, and it encourages legal professionals to specialize in environmental law. As a result, the NGT is recognized as a vital component in the pursuit of environmental justice. Going forward, there is an expectation that environmental legislation will receive increased attention and importance.

The Act permits the creation of committees and bodies to exercise jurisdiction with specific goals, such as the Tiger conservation authority. However, a strong regulatory framework with checks and balances is necessary for effective implementation. The Act must be enforced effectively with a robust infrastructure to protect animals from poaching and killing.

xix. The Wildlife (Protection) Amendment Bill, 2021

The MoEF has presented the Wild Life Amendment Bill, 2021, in the Lok Sabha. Implementing the Convention on International Trade in Endangered Species of Wild Fauna and Flora (CITES) and increasing the number of species covered by this agreement are the main goals of the proposed legislation.

CITES is a treaty between countries to guarantee that the commerce in wild plants and animals does not endanger the extinction of the species. CITES divides plant and animal species into three "Appendices" depending on how likely it is that they will become extinct.

The Agreement mandates that nations use licenses to control the trafficking of all designated specimens. Moreover, it aims to control the ownership of live animal specimens. These CITES requirements are intended to be implemented by the bill.

Some of the key areas the Bill focuses on:-

State Boards of Wildlife Standing Committees: The proposed State Boards of Wildlife Standing Committees would function similarly to the (NBWL) in terms of wildlife management and project licensing. The bill aims to decentralize the process and reduce the burden on the NBWL by allowing State Boards to make decisions on projects that do not require the NBWL's intervention.

These Standing Committees will be established in each state and union territory and will be chaired by the respective Chief Wildlife Warden. The Standing Committees will oversee the implementation of the Wildlife Act, 1972 and the National Wildlife Action Plan. They will also advise the State Governments on matters related to wildlife conservation, and take necessary measures for the protection of wildlife in the state.

Furthermore, the bill proposes to expand the definition of wildlife under the Wildlife Act, 1972 to include aquatic animals and plants, as well as migratory species that are not native to India but pass through the country. This will allow for better protection of these species and their habitats. The proposed amendments also call for stricter penalties for wildlife crimes and an increase in the fines imposed for such violations.

In summary, the Wild Life Amendment Bill, 2021 proposes to establish State Boards of Wildlife Standing Committees to decentralize decision-making on wildlife management and project licensing, expand the definition of wildlife under the Wildlife Act, 1972, and increase penalties for wildlife crimes.

Rationalization of Wildlife Schedules: The reduction in the number of schedules aims to simplify the classification and management of wildlife species under the Act. The two schedules for specially protected animals will differentiate species based on their conservation status and the level of protection they require. The removal of the schedule for vermin species indicates a shift towards more humane methods of managing pest populations. The new schedule for CITES-listed specimens will help ensure that India meets its international obligations to prevent the exploitation of endangered species.

The Bill reduces the number of Wildlife Schedules under the Act from 6 to 4 primary Schedules. There are six schedules for specially protected plants 1, specially protected animals 4, and vermin species 1.

The Wildlife Management Plans, are created for the national parks around the nation, is part of the Wildlife Act, according to the Bill. Also, they require state approval from the Chief Wildlife Warden. As a result, these protected sites receive stricter protection. The proposals had already received executive order approval.

xx. The National Green Tribunal Act, 2010

The National Green Tribunal Act of 2010 was put into effect to provide legal solutions, for individuals impacted by pollution or environmental damage. Established a decade ago the National Green Tribunal (NGT) acts[68] as a specialized court proficient in resolving disputes within the country. Formed based on recommendations from the Supreme Court and the Law Commission and in accordance with India's commitments to create and enforce environmentallaws effectively the NGT serves as a dedicated platform for addressing diverse environmentalissues.

National Green Tribunal (NGT) acts68 as a specialized court proficient in resolving disputes within the country. Formed based on recommendations from the Supreme Court and the Law Commission and in accordance with India's commitments to create and enforce environmental laws effectively the NGT serves as a dedicated platform for addressing diverse environmental issues.

As environmental concerns often intersect with sectors the formation of the NGT ensures that these matters are given attention in specialized settings. The Tribunals jurisdiction includes settling conflicts related to conservation, forest protection and upholding all rights associated with preserving the environment. Its rulings carry weight. Can be enforced, including provisions for granting compensation and other remedies to affected parties.

Furthermore the NGT upholds the right to an environment as outlined in Article 21. Within six months of its establishment all cases brought before it must be adjudicated by the NGT. The Tribunal primarily deals with cases involving concerns. Notably the NGT plays a role in enhancing knowledge in environmental law making it an important avenue, for seeking justice in matters concerning the environment.

With the increasing awareness and significance of laws the National Green Tribunal (NGT) is expected to play a crucial role, in environmental governance.

- The Air (Prevention and Control of Pollution) Act, 1981

    The main goal of the Act is to tackle and control air pollution in India by;-

- Reducing, preventing and handling air pollution.

- Setting up rules, for creating state and central boards to supervise the enforcement of the law. The Central Pollution Control Board (CPCB) and the State Pollution Control Boards (SPCBs) are entrusted with this task.

Rules are set to limit the release of particles, lead, carbon monoxide, sulfur dioxide, nitrogen oxides and volatile organic compounds, into the air from sources like engines, factories, cars and power plants. State authorities are tasked with identifying regions, with air pollution levels.

xxi. The Forest (Conservation) Act, 1980[70]

Forests are a gift, from nature, to humanity. It is everyone's responsibility to protect the environment they provide. However the fast rate of deforestation disrupts cycles. Therefore laws are necessary to ensure forests are preserved. The main goal of the legislation is to protect forests and the wide variety of plants, animals and other living things they support while maintaining the richness and diversity of these ecosystems. Additionally the law prohibits using forest lands for grazing, farming or any commercial purposes.

xxii. The Public Liability Insurance Act and Rules 1991

The enactment of the Public Liability Insurance Act and Rules in 1991, along with the subsequent Amendment in 1992, aimed to facilitate public liability insurance coverage. This insurance provides compensation to individuals in case of accidental harm caused while handling hazardous substances.

xxiii. The Biological Diversity Act, 2002

The main goals of the Act focus, on protecting biodiversity managing its use effectively and ensuring sharing of benefits from usage. It also aims to safeguard knowledge combat biopiracy. Prevent unauthorized patent requests. Sections 36,37 and 38 specifically deal with biodiversity protection by establishing policies and programs identifying biological diversity regions at the state level and giving the central government authority to classify species as critically endangered, endangered or protected from collection. However balancing resource utilization regulations with management principles may pose challenges.

Article 21 governs the distribution of benefits under the Act to ensure compensation, for both resource users and local communities involved in the process. This compensation covers benefits derived from resources, their derivatives, knowledge and related practices.[72]

xxiv. The Noise Pollution (Regulation and Control) (Amendment) Rules, 2010

The main goals of the Act are to protect biodiversity regulate its use, for management and ensure sharing of benefits from its utilization. It also aims to safeguard knowledge combat bio piracy. Prevent unauthorized patent filings. Sections 36,37 and 38 focus on biodiversity protection by setting up policies and programs identifying biological diversity regions at the state level and giving the central government authority to classify species as critically endangered, endangered or protected. However balancing natural resource use regulation with management principles can be challenging.

The regulations specify guidelines for using loudspeakers or public address systems during night cultural events to reduce noise pollution between 10:00 p.m. and mid night.

Key elements of the Amendment include

- Prohibition on using loudspeakers or sound systems after dark except, in emergenciesor indoor settings.

- The highest acceptable volume level, for loudspeakers or public address systems islimited to 75 dB or 10 dB whichever is less.

- In areas horns should only be sounded in case of emergencies.

- Construction equipment that creates noise is not allowed to operate during the night time.

V. Role of judiciary in environmental justice

The judiciary plays a role, in promoting justice worldwide aiming to achieve sustainable development and fair allocation of resources. It acts as a protector of rights interpreting laws resolving conflicts and holding those who harm the environment accountable. Environmental justice is based on principles of fairness, equality and the right to an environment. Judicial interventions aim to address injustices and shield communities from disproportionate harm. Through decisions and evolving legal principles the judiciary shapes environmental governance by upholding public trust in safeguarding natural resources and ensuring fairness between generations. Exploring how the judiciary contributes to environmental justice highlights not the influence of institutions in driving positive change but also the complexities of addressing environmental disputes within a framework of social justice and sustainability. This study aims to examine aspects of how the judiciary promotes justice, impacting policy creation, enforcement strategies and ensuring environmental rights, for everyone.

The Bhopal Gas Tragedy Case of 1986[135] involving Union Carbide Corporation and the Union of India highlighted a concern regarding the development of environmental criminal law. Despite being considered the disaster globally the outcome saw Union Carbide Corporation (UCC) escaping criminal responsibility signaling a troubling beginning, for this legal domain. The court's decision to separate prosecution from proceedings resulted in the termination of the criminal cases. However there were limitations, to the courts authority to halt these proceedings leading to an order that resulted in the dismissal of all charges, including contempt charges and ultimately led to the acquittal of the accused parties.

The legal case known as **M.C. Mehta, v. Union of India (referred to as The Oleum Gas Leak Case)** in [136] 1987 stemmed from a gas leakage incident that occurred after the Bhopal Gas Tragedy. An extensive release of Oleum gas took place at one of the units belonging to Shriram Food and Fertilizer

---

135. M.C. Mehta v. Union of India, (1987) 1 SCC 395.
136. M.C. Mehta v. Union of India, (1987) 1 SCC 395.

Industries leading to harm to both employees and local residents near the factory. Sadly it was reported that a lawyer lost their life due to the gas leak. The court rightfully sought to hold the chairman, Managing Director and other executives accountable for this catastrophe along, with the operator and head of the plant involved. These individuals are often seen as representing the corporation's knowledge, essence and functioning. However the outcome of this case turned out to be quite underwhelming as the Court later modified its decision. As a result the Court stated that officials could avoid liability if they could prove that the gas leak was due, to an Act of God force majeure or sabotage. Despite this setback this case plays a role in shaping the development of law in environmental jurisprudence. Additionally it led to the introduction of the concept of liability in India, which represents a positive advancement, in environmental legal principles.

In **Dwarka Cement Works v. The State of Gujarat (1992)[137]** we see how gaps in the framework allow companies to come up with excuses escaping accountability, for wrongdoings. In this instance the corporation tried using an excuse to avoid being held liable. The Chairman, Director and General Manager involved in the wrongdoing claimed that the accusation did not directly link them to the industry's operations so they should not bear responsibility, for the harm caused. Nevertheless the Court dismissed their assertion denying them the opportunity to escape accountability using strategies.

The legal dispute of **M.C. Mehta, v. Union of India in 2003[138]** marked a victory for activist Mr. M.C. Mehta as he successfully pursued criminal charges against the defendant. The Supreme Court ordered the closure of the defendants hot mix plant unit despite their claims of having High Court approval for their actions. When served with a contempt notice the defendant responded defiantly this time targeting the Apex Court. In reaction to this behavior the Supreme Court aimed to send a message not only to the defendant but also to others discouraging similar conducts in the future. The defendant, held accountable for endangering health through air pollution

---

137. Dwarka Cement Works v. The State of Gujarat, (1992) 2 SCC 4.
138. M.C. Mehta v. Union of India, (2003) 7 SCC 11.

faced penalties including one week of simple imprisonment and fine of one Lakh rupees. While some may view a week's imprisonment as lenient for such an offense this case marked advancement in applying consequences, within environmental law.

i. Challenges and opportunities in judicial Interpretations

The field of interpretation when dealing with injustice and crime is filled with both obstacles and possibilities. One major challenge stems from the nature of issues, which often go beyond national borders and involve complex scientific, technical and socio economic factors. Judges interpreting laws in this realm must navigate a maze of principles, scientific data and conflicting interests, without legislative direction. Moreover the inherent uncertainties and evolving risks associated with the environment make decision making difficult for courts as they grapple with issues like risk assessment, causation and the precautionary principle.

Additionally judicial interpretations encounter difficulties related to ensuring access to justice for marginalized communities disproportionately impacted by harm. Factors such as socio barriers, legal complexities and procedural obstacles often hinder affected individuals and communities' ability to seek justice through the system perpetuating disparities in environmental justice access. Moreover political pressures or vested interests may compromise independence and impartiality undermining the judiciary's effectiveness in resolving disputes and upholding the rule of law.

Nevertheless within these challenges lie opportunities for the judiciary to play a role in fostering change, in the realm of justice.

By using interpretations making landmark judgments and actively engaging in judicial activities courts have the potential to promote environmental sustainability, fairness and responsibility. When courts prioritize safeguarding communities, upholding rights and enforcing the polluter pays principle they establish a strong example, for future environmental legal cases and policy actions.

Furthermore improvements in tools like interest lawsuits, class actions and environmental rights enforcement can increase the accessibility of justice and empower individuals and communities impacted by pollution to hold those responsible accountable. By considering evidence and expert testimonies judges can enhance the credibility and thoroughness of environmental decision making processes to ensure that their interpretations are based on scientific principles and factual data.

In summary despite facing obstacles how courts interpret cases of injustice and wrongdoing offer opportunities for them to make a positive impact on advancing environmental justice and sustainability. Through upholding laws defending rights and promoting access to justice the judiciary can contribute towards creating a more equitable and sustainable future, for everyone.

Chapter 10
Environmental Crime: Types And Patterns

Environmental criminal law deals, with behaviors that violate laws covering both procedural aspects. The United Nations Inter Regional Crime and Justice Research Institute describes crime as a range of unlawful activities, such as wildlife trafficking, illegal trade of ozone depleting substances hazardous waste trafficking, unregulated fishing and unauthorized logging as well as black marketing of Sandalwoods. These actions not harm the environment. Disrupt the balance of ecosystems but also pose challenges to upholding the 'rule of law' within a society. Any activity that negatively impacts quality of life and is not regulated by authorities can hinder an individual's ability to exercise their fundamental 'right to life'.

There is one thing to think about when it comes to the point mentioned earlier which relates to the responsibility of individuals who affect the 'right to life' of victims who may not have a voice like animals or are unknown secondary victims or even faceless victims such as water bodies or glaciers that do not have a 'right to life'. In cases of crimes pinpointing a victim in time can be difficult especially since the effects of an action may not be seen for years leading to victimization across generations.

A good example of offenses is the breach of air pollution regulations. It took a time before we acknowledged the health risks posed by the air released by industries. Despite causing thousands of deaths each year, air pollution is often seen as victimless in terms of crime. This perception and lack of priority often result in responses from governments and enforcement agencies.

Considering these points this document explores how law enforcement agencies in India address crimes. Additionally it sets the foundation for developing law practices in India with a focus, on wildlife violations which rise to the case against environment as wildlife is a part of it.

There is an aspect to think about regarding the point mentioned earlier concerning the responsibility of individuals who affect the 'right to life' of victims who may not have a voice, such as animals or are unknown – referred to as secondary victims or even faceless victims like water bodies or glaciers which do not have a 'right to life'. In cases of crimes identifying a victim in time can be difficult especially considering that the repercussions of an action may not be evident for years resulting in victimization across generations and the surroundings.

An example illustrating offenses is the violation of air pollution regulations. It took an amount of time before we acknowledged the health risks posed by the air released by industries. Despite causing thousands of deaths each year environmental crime is often perceived as victimless. These perceptions of there being no victim and lack of priority often lead governments and enforcement agencies to respond considering these points this paper examines how law enforcement agencies in India address crimes. Additionally it sets the foundation for developing criminal law jurisprudence in India with a focus, on wildlife related offenses.

Wildlife crimes involve victims who cannot advocate for themselves and often rely on animal rights activists for representation. Activities falling under this category, like the illicit trafficking of birds and animals are commonly carried out by organized groups that operate internationally. A quick review of cases recorded on the Wildlife Crime Control Bureaus (referred to as WCCB) website highlights the participation of individuals from Myanmar and Bangladesh in smuggling animals and their body parts across borders. The attraction of rewards combined with the perceived low risk of getting caught serves as a major incentive for potential offenders to participate in such illegal activities. As, per a report released by the Environmental Investigation Agency (EIA) the wildlife trade industry is estimated to be worth billions of dollars.

Government and non-government entities, like the Wildlife Crime Control Bureau (WCCB) Environmental Investigation Agency (EIA) and United Nations Environment Programme (UNEP) are actively involved in environmental law enforcement. Additionally organizations such as the Wildlife Trust of India (WTI) People for the Ethical Treatment of Animals

(PETA) and World Wide Fund for Nature (WWF) focus on wildlife conservation through community initiatives. Despite their approaches both groups share an objective; to uphold environmental justice for all.

Environmental justice entails ensuring protection under laws without discrimination based on race, ethnicity or socio economic status. It emphasizes treatment and inclusive participation in developing and enforcing policies, for everyone regardless of background. This discussion specifically delves into the implementation and enforcement of laws concerning wildlife protection within the realm of law. Numerous governmental and non-governmental entities, such, as the Wildlife Crime Control Bureau (WCCB) the Environmental Investigation Agency (EIA) and the United Nations Environment Programme (UNEP) actively participate in environmental law enforcement. Similarly organizations like the Wildlife Trust of India (WTI) People for the Ethical Treatment of Animals (PETA) and the World Wide Fund for Nature (WWF) are dedicated to wildlife preservation and conservation through community initiatives. Despite their approaches both sets of organizations share an objective; ensuring environmental justice for all.

Environmental justice entails advocating for rights and safeguards under legislation without bias based on race, ethnicity or economic status. It promotes treatment and inclusive involvement of all individuals regardless of their background or income level in shaping and upholding policies. This article focuses specifically on implementing and enforcing laws related to wildlife protection, within the realm of law.

There are two ways to deal with issues; (i) the socio legal approach which involves using civil courts and (ii) environmental criminal law, which focuses on punishing those who violate environmental laws. While both methods aim to reduce harm to the environment they have ways of working.

Civil environmental law follows principles like the polluter pays principle, principle and public trust doctrine. On the hand environmental criminal law deals with making certain actions illegal and penalizing those who break the rules.

Environmental criminal law respects all aspects of justice. This includes ensuring a trial, for defendants presuming innocence until proven guilty and requiring the prosecution to prove its case as established by court decisions.

Moreover laws governing crimes also adhere to the rule of law. Individuals accused of harming the environment can only be punished according to procedures, in place with all their rights protected by the constitution. Penalties set out in these laws are appropriate based on the seriousness of the offense.

Penal law operates based on three principles of punishment; retributive, deterrence and compensatory. In law the civil courts typically handle the aspect while criminal courts focus on applying retributive or deterrence theories of punishment.

Retributive punishment involves inflicting suffering on the offender that's proportional, to what the victim endured. However in crimes determining the nature of suffering and quantifying the harm caused to nature or society can be complex. Hence it may be challenging to apply the theory in criminal cases. While it is not definitive if the punitive actions in environmental criminal law align with deterrence theory it seems to be a choice in this scenario.[139]

Deterrence aims to discourage offenses by penalizing wrongdoers in a way that dissuades offenders. As emphasized by H.L.A. Hart considerations like crime prevention are crucial in punishment; however punishment must follow the principle that only those proven guilty should face consequences commensurate, with their offenses.

It is essential for procedures to uphold due process rights. This aspect is a focus of India's criminal justice systems efforts. It is as fair and just, as any criminal justice system.

---

139. Lynch, Michael J., Stretesky, Paul B., and Long, Michael A. "Green Criminology: Crime, Justice, and the Environment." University of California Press, 2017

The Indian Parliament passed laws, like the Wildlife Protection Act of 1972 the Air (Prevention and Control of Pollution) Act of 1974 the Water (Prevention and Control of Pollution) Act of 1981 and the Environment Protection Act of 1986. These laws aim to make actions that harm or could harm the environment, including surroundings illegal. In today's world where environmental concerns widespread, it is essential to enforce these laws to achieve their objectives effectively.

In this context this paper explores aspects of environmental criminal law jurisprudence such as trials, adherence to legal principles fairness in environmental matters and the concept of deterrence in punishment under environmental criminal law. The paper aims to address questions; (i) How well do law enforcement bodies ensure trials while upholding legal principles for environmental offenses like wildlife crimes? (ii) What is the duration of trials, for offenses? (iii) Does a swift trial guarantee outcomes in cases? (iv) are punishment and expedited trials effective, in deterring crimes a goal of the criminal justice system, for the environment?

In this paper we delve into the analysis of criminal law with a focus, on wildlife related violations. The main goal of highlighting data is to; (i) evaluate the implementation of environmental laws, (ii) collect information on the prosecution of criminal cases (iii) document details on case processing and resolution and (iv) compile data on conviction and acquittal rates, in such cases.

I. Cases Regarding the Reporting of Offenses Committed under Environmental Protection Laws

Once a report is made the legal system springs, into action. It is expected that law enforcement agencies trust the informants account of the crime as valid and accurate. When an incident is reported the information shared by the informant is considered reliable. Their understanding of the situation is seen as accurate. The following data outlines the details regarding reports of violations-

In the reports of the National Crime Records Bureau (NCRB) data shows that there were a total of 34,671 cases of crimes reported in 2019. The number of reported incidents has gradually decreased over the three years. In 2017 and 2018 the numbers stood at 42,143 and 35,196 respectively. The corresponding crime rates, for these years also dropped to 3.3, 2.7 and 2.6 in 2017, 2018 and 2019 respectively. A notable increase was seen from 4,732 incidents in 2016 to a figure of 42,143 in one year. Before this peak in reporting occurred in 2017 the average number of reported incidents was around the mark of 5,000.[140]

It is worth mentioning that before the year 2016 environmental violations were not separately listed in NCRB reports. Furthermore starting from the year 2017 NCRB began including offenses under the Cigarette and Other Tobacco Products Act as part of violations – a category that was not accounted for prior to this period. This change resulted in a surge in reported data, for the year specifically marked as '2017'.

The number of reported wildlife crimes has been, on a trend over the four years from 859 incidents in 2016 to 826, 782 and 618 in the subsequent years. Despite this decline wildlife offenses still account for around 2% of all crimes during this period. This indicates that the drop in reporting wildlife crimes is not as significant as, for violations. It implies that the factors leading to reduced reporting of crimes may not be as effective when it comes to reporting wildlife offenses.

The data also shows that the average number of arrests, per case for wildlife offenses was 1.8 in 2017 (1497 arrests in 826 reported cases) which reduced to 1.65 in 2018 (1295 arrests in 782 reported cases). Then slightly increased to 1.75 in 2019 (1087 arrests in 618 reported cases). On the hand for all offenses the average arrests per case were at 0.96 in 2017 (40,720 arrests in 42,143 reported cases) rose to 1.06 in 201885 (37,408 arrests in 35,196 reported cases) and remained stable at around 1.04 in 2019 (36,237 arrests in 34,671 reported cases).[141]

Wildlife crimes often involve organized activities and multiple individuals participating in the offense compared to violations which might involve fewer people per case leading to a higher average number of arrests. Furthermore

---

140. National Crime Records Bureau (NCRB), Crime in India Report 2019
141. National Crime Records Bureau (NCRB), Crime in India Report (2017, 2018, 2019)

when dealing with crimes law enforcement agencies face challenges arresting suspects outside India's border. This raises a question; does a higher arrest rate correlate with a conviction rate?

Criminal proceedings can only commence once an incident is reported; therefore maintaining accurate and truthful records of incidents is crucial. Any analysis of data, like charge sheeting rates or conviction/acquittal rates relies heavily on the reporting of incidents. Since 2017 the NCRB has begun including crimes, in a chapter, in their reports. Furthermore the information disclosed in NCRB documents indicate that proper records of violations were not consistently kept up until recent times.

II. Nature of Environmental Crime

In the thirty years following the United Nations Conference, on the Human Environment held in Stockholm in 1972 over 250 international and regional agreements concerning environmental issues have been put into place. These accords have progressed beyond displays of cooperation to include practical regulations such as trade limitations with the goal of effectively tackling environmental problems. Nevertheless as these measures are enforced there has been an increase in efforts to circumvent compliance. This comprehensive structure highlights the recognition of the connection, between development and the environment incorporating environmental preservation within regulatory frameworks. The idea is captured in a concept of law called sustainable development. The known definition, as presented in the 1987 Brundtland report explains that sustainable development involves fulfilling the generation's needs without compromising the ability of future generations to fulfill their own needs.

Environmental crimes are now viewed as serious societal wrongdoings, to offences. The main motivation, behind these crimes, which go against agreements, is typically financial profit. The common traits associated with crimes are sadly familiar; networks, porous borders, illegal migration, money laundering, corruption and the exploitation of vulnerable communities. Individuals involved in wildlife crime exhibit a level of cruelty as criminals using intimidation, human rights violations, impunity, violence and even murder in their activities. The impacts of crimes can be seen across sectors of international development efforts. These criminal activities contribute to challenges addressed by initiatives, like the Millennium Development Goals (MDGs) exacerbating issues related to development progress, peacekeeping efforts, security measures and human rights protection. The persistent problems are starting to get noticed more with authorities, around the globe beginning to recognize the role of organized crime in offenses. It's becoming increasingly clear that illegal logging and wildlife traffics are frequently carried out by groups taking advantage of resources resulting in habitat loss. This not impacts communities' means of living but also Weakens the overall economy and presents a significant danger, to endangered species and ecosystems.

Scholars have been studying the aspects of crimes. For example White and Heckenberg discuss types of concerns; urban issues (brown) wilderness conservation (green) and the impact of new technologies, like GMOs (white). These offenses can be committed by individuals, groups, governments or businesses. Currently there is no agreement specifically addressing harm. The main reference point in this field is the UN Environment Programmes guidelines from 2010, which focus on liability response actions and compensation for damage caused by activities, to the environment. According to these guidelines environmental damage can result from not following requirements or from reckless or negligent behaviors.[142]

In contrast, to crimes like theft and robbery that involve taking existing wealth without consent, environmental crime deals with the production and distribution of goods and services which are illegal in nature. This type of activity is more akin to a market structure than a display of deviance. It involves exchanges among producers, processors, sellers and buyers where there is a demand for services, in a free market setting. The typical law enforcement approach of targeting wrongdoers overlooks the dynamics of supply and demand that drive profit opportunities. In contrast, to crimes focused on stealing wealth through theft and robbery environmental crime involves the production and

---

142. White, Rob, and Heckenberg, Diane. *Green Criminology: An Introduction to the Study of Environmental Harm.* Routledge, 2014

distribution of goods and services. This type of activity operates like a market than a display of social deviance with organized exchanges among producers, processors, retailers and consumers in a free market setting. The typical law enforcement approach of targeting offenders overlooks the supply and demand dynamics that drive profitability within this realm.

Environmental offenses have reaching impacts on the environment and future generations compared to crimes. Actions such as deforestation, chemical dumping and illegal fishing harm ecosystem services like air, water quality, weather stability, food security, health and wellbeing. Furthermore they hinder government revenues and legitimate businesses. These crimes often transcend borders. Are coordinated by criminal groups due, to global trade facilitating illicit activities in todays interconnected world.

III. The Criminal Liability

The Environmental Protection Act of 1986 was put into effect in March. Officially started on November 19, 1986 after the Bhopal Gas incident. This legislation was sanctioned under Article 253 of the Indian Constitution. Comprises 26 Sections categorized into, around 4 Chapters. Known as a law the Environmental Protection Act aims to synchronize the actions of both the State governments drawing its power from the Water (Prevention and Control) Act of 1974 and the Air (Prevention and Control) Act of 1981.

This law establishes a set of rules and fundamental principles to manage actions impacting the environment. It emphasizes combatting pollution as an aspect of its implementation strategies. In countries like India environmental regulations primarily tackle issues such as air and water pollution, waste disposal, preservation of forests and soil quality as promoting sustainable development. Grasping the essence of legislation. Ensuring its enforcement is vital, in addressing environmental offenses.

There are types of offenses, like;

- Wildlife Crime- Wildlife crime is an issue globally linked to organized criminal activities. This illegal practice involves the hunting, trading or smuggling of animal species or their parts, for profit. Regions like

Latin America, Africa and Asia are known hotspots, for wildlife crime according to the IUCN. The impact of this behavior extends to a range of wildlife including mammals, birds, reptiles, amphibians, insects and plants.

- Illegal hunting or poaching

- Smuggling wildlife or plants for profit such as the unlawful trading of wood, ivory, rhino horns, etc.

- Transporting wild animals illegally and Undeclared fishing practices- Unauthorized fishing, also known as fishing involves foreign ships fishing without permission, in waters or breaking fisheries laws. This often happens in waters or within countries.

- Exclusive Economic Zone (EEZ). The Indian government has introduced a bill to monitor fishing activities beyond its waters and combat illegal fishing in the EEZ. According to the proposed law state governments will be responsible, for granting fishing licenses within the EEZ.

- Uncontrolled logging- Unauthorized tree cutting, known as logging involves breaking established laws. This activity includes the collection, transportation, processing, buying or selling of timber, in defiance of international rules. Studies by the International Union of Forest Research Organizations reveal that illegal logging is widespread worldwide and significantly affects forest areas. China, India and Vietnam are the importers of illegal tropical wood products. Due to illicit logging and land encroachment the Keo Seima Wildlife Sanctuary in Cambodia has lost, around 5% of its forest cover since 2010.

- Improper disposal of electronic waste

- Dumping waste, in rivers or groundwater sources

- Incorrect use of pesticides

Chapter XIV of the Indian Penal Code of 1860 focuses on offenses related to health andsafety.

- Under Section 268 environmental offenses are classified as nuisances.

- Section 290 addresses the offense of causing a nuisance.

- Activities that lead to water pollution are penalized under Section 277 with the possibility of imprisonment.

- Section 278 specifies punishment, for harming the environment in a way that endangers someone's health.

- Punishment for causing pollution through mischief is enforced under Section 426.

- Under Section 430 individuals can face penalties for causing a decrease in water supply for use human consumption or animal welfare.

- Engaging in actions that make any public road, bridge, navigable river or channel impassable or unsafe, for travel or property conveyance can lead to punishment under Section 431.

- Similarly actions that cause flooding or obstruct public drainage systems leading to injury or damage can result in penalties under Section 432.

Rules that hold individuals accountable, for protecting the environment

- Section 133 of the Code of Criminal Procedure (CrPC) gives power to a district magistrate and sub divisional magistrate to stop any kind of disturbance.

- Under Section 47 of the Water Act individuals can be held responsible, for crimes committed by a company if they are, in charge of the companies business activities.

- Similarly Section 16 imposes accountability in situations.

IV. Case studies of Environmental Crimes

a) Bhopal Gas Tragedy (1984);[143]

One of the ecological catastrophes, in history the Bhopal Gas Tragedy unfolded when a pesticide factory owned by Union Carbide Corporation released methyl isocyanate gas exposing more than half a million individuals to harmful fumes. This event resulted in fatalities and lasting health issues for survivors. Investigations uncovered lapses in safety protocols and inadequate plant upkeep leading to accusations of negligence and environmental offenses against Union Carbide and its executives.

The Bhopal Gas Tragedy, in 1984 is remembered as one of the disasters in history causing significant harm to human health and the environment. It took place on December 3rd, 1984 when a pesticide plant owned by Union Carbide Corporation (UCC) in Bhopal, India released around 40 tons of methyl isocyanine (MIC) gas into the air. This deadly gas spread across the city of Bhopal exposing than half a million individuals to its lethal effects.

Following the gas leak there was chaos and confusion as residents hurried to escape from their homes to avoid the fumes. The impact of the tragedy was immense with thousands losing their lives within days due to gas exposure and tens of thousands experiencing issues, eye irritation, neurological problems and other health complications. The lack of preparedness and inadequate emergency response worsened the situation as hospitals struggled to handle the number of patients.

Investigations, into the Bhopal Gas Tragedy uncovered a series of failures and negligence on the part of UCC and its Indian subsidiary, Union Carbide India Limited (UCIL).The safety measures, at the plant were discovered to be severely lacking with reports indicating corroded storage tanks, faulty safety gear and insufficient staff training. Additionally essential maintenance and repairs were neglected in

---

143. Union Carbide Corporation v. Union of India, AIR 1990 SC 273.

favor of cost saving strategies jeopardizing the effectiveness of safety systems.

Following the disaster Union Carbide and its representatives faced a wave of accusations and civil lawsuits both domestically and internationally. The Indian government pressed charges against UCC and UCIL for alleged homicide and negligence leading to fatalities. However legal proceedings were drawn out. Shrouded in controversy as UCC aimed to downplay its responsibility and avoid being held accountable for the incident. In 1989 a contentious settlement was reached between UCC and the Indian government where $470 million was agreed upon as compensation, for victims a fraction of the estimated damages.

Despite these resolutions the repercussions of the Bhopal Gas Tragedy continue to afflict survivors and their families who have endured years of ailments, emotional distress and financial challenges. Furthermore the environmental impacts persist with soil and groundwater posing health threats to nearby communities.

The Bhopal Gas Tragedy serves as an example of how corporate irresponsibility can have consequences, on people highlighting the importance of strong regulations, corporate responsibility and fair treatment of the environment, in industrial activities.

b) **Niger Delta Oil Pollution;**

The Niger Delta region, in Nigeria has faced challenges due to oil pollution caused by corporations engaging in oil extraction activities over several decades. A notable case is the pollution of Ogoniland by Royal Dutch Shell, a player in the regions oil industry. The continuous occurrence of oil spills, pipeline leaks and gas flaring has had consequences in Ogoniland impacting the wellbeing and livelihoods of local residents.

Best Ordinioha and Saiyefa Brisibe, The human health implications of crude oil spills in the Niger delta, Nigeria: An interpretation of published studies

The effects of oil pollution in Ogoniland are extensive leading to harm to land, water sources and biodiversity. Rivers, creeks and fishing areas have been contaminated by oil spills disrupting the communities traditional means of sustenance and income generation. Additionally the hazardous chemicals released during these incidents have seeped into the ground making agricultural lands infertile and unsuitable for farming. The loss of soil and clean water has worsened poverty levels and food insecurity in Ogoniland perpetuating a cycle of hardship.

Despite growing evidence of harm and community concerns regarding oil pollution in Ogoniland efforts to address these issues have encountered obstacles such, as resistance and delays. Royal Dutch Shell has been accused of negligence, inadequate infrastructure maintenance practices and delays in responding to oil spill incidents.

Furthermore the involvement of government officials and regulatory bodies, in supporting oil extraction activities without protections has worsened the environmental issues in the Niger Delta.

In response to increasing pressure from impacted communities and non-governmental organizations the Nigerian government launched the Ogoni Environmental Restoration Project in 2006. This initiative aimed to evaluate the damage in Ogoni land and implement actions. However progress has been sluggish and effective remediation efforts have yet to be realized leaving Ogoniland communities struggling with the lasting effects of oil contamination.

The situation of oil pollution in the Niger Delta highlights the importance of holding corporations accountable, reforming regulations and empowering communities to address environmental injustices. It underscores how environmental degradation, human rights violations and socio economic disparities are interconnected in resource areas like the Niger Delta. Resolving the crisis of oil pollution in the Niger

Delta necessitates an approach involving companies, government entities, non-governmental organizations and affected communities to promote environmental sustainability, social equity and human dignity, in the region.

The Niger Delta area in Nigeria has endured years of oil spills and pollution stemming from oil extraction activities conducted by corporations. Instances like the pollution of Ogoniland by Royal Dutch Shell showcase the harm caused by oil spills, including harm to agricultural land, water sources and wildlife diversity. The absence of cleanup actions and compensation for impacted communities has sparked claims of transgressions and violations of human rights against oil firm's active, in the region.

c)   Oleum Gas Leak Case (1985):

One of the most infamous industrial disasters in India, the leakage of oleum gas from the Union Carbide plant in Bhopal resulted in thousands of deaths and injuries. The incident ledto criminal charges against the company officials, including the CEO Warren Anderson. Although Anderson was initially arrested, he was released on bail and left the country, evading imprisonment. However, several Indian officials faced charges, with some being sentenced to prison terms.

The Oleum Gas Leak Case of 1985 stands as one of the most catastrophic industrial disasters in Indian history, epitomizing the devastating consequences of negligence in industrial safety and environmental management. The incident occurred at the Union Carbide pesticide plant in Bhopal, Madhya Pradesh, on the night of December 2-3, 1984, when methyl isocyanate (MIC) gas, along with other toxic chemicals, leaked from a storage tank, engulfing the surrounding areas in a deadly cloud of gas.

The leak resulted in the deaths of thousands of people and left countless others with debilitating injuries and long-term health complications. The immediate aftermath saw scenes of chaos and suffering as overwhelmed hospitals struggled to cope with the influx of victims suffering from respiratory distress, eye irritation, and other symptoms of chemical exposure. The exact death toll remains a subject of debate, with estimates ranging from several thousand to over 15,000 fatalities.

The aftermath of the disaster was marked by widespread outrage and calls for justice, both within India and internationally. Investigations revealed a series of systemic failures and lapses in safety protocols at the Union Carbide plant, including inadequate maintenance, lack of emergency preparedness, and disregard for environmental regulations. Moreover, allegations of corporate negligence and cost-cutting measures further fueled public anger and demands for accountability.

In the legal realm, the Indian government filed criminal charges against the officials of Union Carbide, including the then-CEO Warren Anderson. However, the pursuit of justice faced numerous obstacles, including legal delays, bureaucratic hurdles, and challenges in extraditing Anderson to India to face trial. Ultimately, Anderson was arrested in India but was released on bail and subsequently left the country, evading imprisonment.

d) Bellandur Lake Pollution Case (2018)[144]:

Bellandur Lake, in Bengaluru became well known for its pollution due to sewage and industrial waste. In 2018 the Karnataka High Court acknowledged the problem. Instructed the state government to address the issue by cleaning up the lake and stopping additional pollution. Following this officials, from the government and regulatory bodies who failed to comply with laws were made answerable leading to some individuals being given prison sentences for contributing to the deterioration of Bellandur Lakes pollution levels.

In 2018 the pollution issue, at Bellandur Lake highlighted India's growing concern over water pollution and the pressing need for action to combat deterioration. Situated in Bengaluru, Karnataka, Bellandur Lake once a pristine water source, had sadly transformed into a symbol

---

144. Bengaluru Paryavaran Vidhyarthi Trust v. State of Karnataka, (2018) 4 Kar. LJ 111.

of neglect and decay due to pollution from sewage and industrial waste. The lake was covered in foam, gases and unsightly debris posing serious health risks to the public and the surrounding environment.

Responding to outcry and legal action taken by citizens and environmental advocates the Karnataka High Court stepped in to address the dire state of Bellandur Lake and its impact on both nature and public 93well being. Through rulings the court directed state authorities and local officials to take immediate steps to combat pollution at Bellandur Lake and restore its ecological balance.

The courts directives included measures such as setting up sewage treatment facilities redirecting sewage inflows away from the lake and enforcing strict regulations on industrial waste disposal into the water body. Additionally there was an emphasis on establishing monitoring systems and enforcement protocols to ensure adherence to standards and hold accountable those responsible, for polluting activities.

Following the courts involvement government officials and authorities who neglected regulations and failed to safeguard Bellandur Lake were held responsible, for their actions. Some officials faced consequences, including imprisonment for contributing to the lakes pollution and breaching laws.

The Bellandur Lake pollution case serves as a reminder of the dangers of deterioration and emphasizes the importance of strong legal frameworks to hold those accountable for contaminating water bodies and jeopardizing public health. It also highlights how judicial activism can address issues and promote development practices. Nonetheless it underscores the need, for efforts to prevent pollution incidents and ensure the lasting rehabilitation and protection of India's water resources.

V. Global And Regional Trends

The issue of crime, on a regional scale highlights the various illegal activities that jeopardize both the environment and human health. Factors like growth unlawful extraction of resources, wildlife trafficking and weak enforcement of environmental laws contribute to the challenge. Illegal logging remains a problem in areas such as the Amazon rainforest and Southeast Asia leading to deforestation loss of habitats and a decline in biodiversity. The illicit trade in wildlife products like ivory rhino horn and exotic pets poses risks to endangered species and ecosystems worldwide.

Apart from crimes new trends like e-waste trafficking, illegal fishing and fraud in carbon emissions trading are becoming more prevalent. Improper disposal of waste in developing nations violates rules and poses health hazards. Illegal fishing practices harm resources and undermine efforts, for fisheries management. Moreover fraudulent activities exploiting carbon trading mechanisms designed to combat climate change expose weaknesses in governance frameworks.

In parts of the world illegal activities that harm the environment take shapes due, to local conditions, economic factors and rules in place. For example in Africa the unlawful trafficking of wildlife items like elephant tusks and pangolin scales poses a danger to animals while undermining conservation efforts. In Asia widespread unauthorized logging and encroachment on land contribute to deforestation and damage to forests worsening harm and sparking disputes over resources.

In Latin America illicit mining operations often connected to organized crime harm ecosystems by polluting water sources and displacing communities highlighting the overlap between issues and social justice concerns. Although environmental crimes at regional levels pose challenges they emphasize the critical need for collaborative efforts involving multiple sectors to tackle the underlying causes and reduce the impacts of illegal actions on nature and society. Strengthened international collaboration improved frameworks; initiatives for building capacity and engaging with communities are crucial, for combatting crimes and fostering sustainable progress. By addressing crimes across all aspects stakeholders can strive towards preserving ecosystems safeguarding biodiversity and ensuring a healthy future for generations to come .

Social aspects also influence conduct by factors like poverty, inequality and lack of access to sustainable livelihoods. In communities facing marginalization and limited economic prospects engaging in practices such as poaching, illegal mining and encroaching on land may be viewed as necessary for survival. Furthermore socio cultural elements like customs and beliefs can impact attitudes towards preservation and resource management. Either supporting or hindering illegal actions.

Insufficient governance structures and enforcement mechanisms worsen the prevalence of crimes by creating opportunities, for abuse and evasion of accountability. Flawed regulatory frameworks, corruption issues and regulatory capture weaken the efficacy of environmental laws and enforcement bodies paving the way for wrongdoers to operate without consequences.

Furthermore failures, within institutions like the lack of coordination among law enforcement agencies and inadequate resources for monitoring and enforcement lead to loopholes that enable activities and impede efforts to combat environmental crime.

Global dynamics also play a role in shaping behavior. This includes crime networks, illicit trade routes and limited international cooperation. Organized crime groups take advantage of borders, regulatory oversight and disjointed legal systems to carry out environmental crimes such as wildlife trafficking and illegal resource extraction on a global scale. Additionally the interconnected nature of challenges like climate change and biodiversity loss highlights the importance of international actions to tackle the underlying causes and lessen the impacts of environmental criminal acts.

In essence various economic, social, institutional and global factors influence behavior. Dealing with these root causes calls, for strategies that combine measures, regulations, economic incentives and social initiatives to promote sustainable development enhance governance structures and encourage responsible environmental practices. By addressing the issues behind offenses stakeholders can strive towards a fairer more inclusive future that prioritizes sustainability for all.

VI. The Ongoing Shift, in how Investigative Agencies Manage Cases

After an issue is reported to the agency they have the choice to either launch an investigation or not. If they decide against investigating they must provide an explanation, for their decision. It is crucial for investigations to be carried out promptly to prevent evidence destruction and witnesses from becoming detached from the process. The data below delves into how the investigative agency plays a role, in ensuring justice delivery while upholding essential criminal law principles.

When a crime is reported the investigating agency looks into it. Presents its findings. They might determine that no crime took place that a crime was committed with evidence to prove the guilt of the accused or that a crime occurred but there wasn't evidence despite their best efforts. According to data, from the NCRB in cases of wildlife crimes it's common not to gather evidence. Specifically in 2016 out of 604 reports where evidence was lacking 19% (115) were related to wildlife offenses. In the following years. 2017, 2018 and 2019. These percentages were 24.6% (96 out of 389) 18.4% (91 out of 493) and 21.9% (68 out of 310).[145]

It's interesting to note that while wildlife offenses make up 2% of all environmental crimes reported during these years around one fifth of investigations end without enough evidence being found in them. One possible explanation for this lack of evidence could be due, to the border nature often associated with wildlife crimes.

When illegal wildlife trade is involved Indian investigating agencies face challenges if the traded products have already passed the border. They cannot cross the border for evidence collection. Nor can they question witnesses from the side. This data provides information, about how the investigation agency submits charge sheets. The rate of charge sheets is determined by the number of cases awaiting investigation and the number of charge sheets filed in a given year. A lower rate suggests an investigation period. Data from NCRB shows

---

145. National Crime Records Bureau (NCRB), Crime in India Report (2016, 2017, 2018, 2019)

that the charge sheet rate for wildlife crimes is lower compared to offenses overall.

Specifically it was 90.4 versus 98.1 in 2015 79.6 versus 82.5 in 2016 83.6 versus 98.4 in 2017 82.8 versus 98.1 in 2018 and 84.2 versus 98.6 in 2019 indicating that wildlife crimes take longer to investigate than offenses.[146]

One reason for these investigations could be the aspect of wildlife crimes and their secretive nature. In cases where victims cannot speak up and offenses occur far from settlements getting witnesses can be difficult. Despite pending cases at the police level the charge sheet rate for wildlife crimes has risen from 79.6 in 2016 to reach up, to around 84 by 2019.[147]

When we look at how many cases are open at the investigation agency we see a trend. The agencies rate of pending cases is calculated by comparing the number of cases in a year to the total number of cases closed by the agency including those closed with a final report. If the agency finds that no crime was committed or if there wasn't evidence collected even if a crime did occur they send a report to suggest closing the case. Data, from NCRB shows that wildlife offense investigations tend to have cases compared to environmental offenses. For example in 2016 it was 34.8 for wildlife offenses versus 22.1 for all offenses. In 2017 it was 27.3 compared to 13.9; in 2018 it was 28.1 compared to 15.2. In 2019 it was 30.8, versus 17.9.[148]

Based on data, from the NCRB it was found that in 2019 out of a total of 542 charge sheets filed by the investigation agency for wildlife offenses 61.2% (332 out of 542) were submitted within the statutory limit of 90 days. This suggests that in 38.2% of cases where investigations were completed in 2019 the statutory time limit was exceeded. Similarly in the years 2018 and 2017

---

146. National Crime Records Bureau (NCRB), India. *Crime in India 2015–2019 Reports.* Government of India

147. Wildlife Crime Control Bureau (WCCB), India. *Annual Report 2019-2020.* Government of India

148. National Crime Records Bureau (NCRB), India. *Crime in India 2016–2019 Reports.* Government of India.

the corresponding percentages stood at 64% (426 out of 665) and 63.4% (473, out of 745) respectively.[149]

VII. Drawback in the Existing Framework to Deal with Environmental Crimes in India

The reasons, behind crimes are varied. Need careful consideration when developing appropriate responses. These causes mainly arise from factors like risks and high profits in regulatory settings as well as governance issues and widespread corruption. Insufficient funding for law enforcement organizations, courts and prosecution coupled with a lack of support, political meddling and low morale among employees also contribute to the problem. Furthermore the absence of benefits for communities and increasing demand in regions such as Asia worsen the situation.

One major concern is the lack of support for prosecution and judicial systems in developing countries. Poverty plays a role by making it easier to recruit individuals at grassroots levels to commit these crimes. Addressing this issue requires an approach that goes beyond enforcing laws. Despite efforts there is still a gap in effectively combating the rising impact of environment related crimes, on funding conflicts and threatening development and environmental security.

In addition the resources allocated to enforcement initiatives targeting crimes are insufficient to effectively control their spread. International bodies such, as INTERPOL, UNEP, WCO, UNODC along with related agreements focusing on combating crimes receive a total funding of approximately 20 to 30 million USD collectively (pending precise calculations). The constrained financial support contributes to the increasing participation of organized crime groups due to regulations. Resolving this challenge requires allocating

---

149. Wildlife Crime Control Bureau (WCCB), India. *Annual Report 2017-2020.* Government of India. This report might also reference data on the procedural timelines followed in wildlife crime investigations.

resources and enhancing collaboration, among agencies to combat these illegal activities.[150]

While laws have made strides in addressing the issue of wildlife trade a key challenge arises from the absence of definitions, for "exotic species" or "exotic pets" within Indian legislation. The guidelines outlined in the Prevention of Cruelty to Animals (Pet Shop) Rules 2016 focus on defining " animals ". This framework is limited to specific animals like dogs, cats, rabbits, guinea pigs, hamsters, certain rodents and captive birds.[151] As a result many exotic species such as turtles, snakes, iguanas, monkeys and others commonly brought into India are not covered by this definition. The Wildlife (Protection) Act 1972 is designed to combat smuggling and illegal trade in wildlife and its derivatives as a goal. However a notable limitation of this law is that it only provides protection for animals listed in its Schedule which are predominantly native to the subcontinent. Exotic species fall outside the scope of this legislation. This gap allows unregulated trade to persist unchecked with penalties applicable to those involved in trading or smuggling scheduled species not being enforceable, in these scenarios.

India has made progress, in managing Ozone Depleting Substances (ODS). Yet the current laws and regulations, in place lack the required strictness to adequately tackle the consequences of ODS. Therefore enacting a law tailored to address this issue would be a fitting resolution.

In February 2017 the Supreme Court criticized the Union Government for allowing foreign waste to be brought into India for recycling and reprocessing only to end up in our landfills. This was seen as harmful, to both people's health and the environment[152]. Following the updated Other Wastes (Management and Tran boundary Movement) Rules of 2016 India had banned importing plastic waste, cooking oils, animal fats and household waste to avoid worsening

---

150. INTERPOL and UNEP. *Strategic Report: Environment, Peace, and Security – A Convergence of Threats*, 2016.

151. Prevention of Cruelty to Animals (Pet Shop) Rules, 2016, Government of India.

152. Research Foundation for Science, Technology and Ecology v. Union of India (2017) 4 SCC 742

our countries waste management issues. The revised laws of 2016 state that operators of facilities handling waste could face fines or imprisonment if they neglect their duties regarding transporting, storing and recycling materials. Additionally these regulations require state government to identify areas, for building plants dedicated to managing waste effectively. Since the new regulations came into effect there haven't been any facilities built specifically for treating waste in India. Currently 17 disposal sites, with secured landfills and proper incinerators are operational across the country. States like Karnataka, Kerala, Punjab and Orissa are facing challenges due to the lack of waste disposal options for materials. The insufficient infrastructure for disposing and recycling waste has led to poor handling practices in India. The practice of burning waste in landfills is still common. Poses significant risks to health and the Environment. Hazardous waste is often not segregated properly during collection and transportation processes leading to recycling efforts. The lack of incineration facilities worsens the situation pushing some collectors to resort to burning waste at temperatures. Additionally those tasked with collecting waste are typically ill prepared undertrained and inadequately compensated. These workers frequently face exposure to substances, in hazardous materials resulting in serious health issues. Moreover they often lack the tools to handle waste safely.

When it comes to unregulated and unreported (IUU) fishing the current governmental regulations and legislations fall short. The poverty faced by fishermen worsens this problem. Even the Fisheries Policy of 2020 does not effectively address IUU fishing in India. Furthermore the immediate elimination of the Letter of Permit policy is necessary to fight against IUU fishing in the nation.[153]

---

153. CMFRI (Central Marine Fisheries Research Institute). *India's Marine Fisheries Policies: Status and Recommendations*, 2020

Navigating The Intersection of Environmentalcrime And Concerns of Indigenous People

Tribal communities in India, known as Adivasis, represent groups of people who share a common ancestry and cultural heritage, often choosing to live in close-knit, self-contained societies. They make up a significant portion of the Indian population and play an essential role in the country's rich, intangible cultural heritage.

Historically, Adivasis have been deeply connected to their natural environment, relying on forests and ecosystems for their livelihoods. There are over 700 recognized tribes listed under Article 342 of the Indian Constitution, and these indigenous groups are spread across the nation. Living in harmony with nature, Adivasis maintain a simple way of life, untouched by the artificiality that is often associated with urban living. They typically inhabit remote forests and mountainous areas, far removed from the hustle and bustle of cities.

As the original inhabitants of India, Adivasis should be acknowledged as 'indigenous peoples' who safeguard a wealth of cultural traditions, including distinct languages, food practices, art forms, dance, music, and spiritual beliefs. These traditions reflect a deep connection with nature and a strong communal bond. Tribal cultures are marked by their unique social structures and spiritual systems, with each community contributing its own strengths to the broader society.

For instance, many tribal groups possess a deep knowledge of herbal medicine, while others excel in handicrafts or sustainable agricultural practices.

The Adivasis of the Northeast are known for their matrilineal society and vibrant oral traditions, while the Bhils of central India have honed water conservation techniques and live closely aligned with the natural environment. The Gonds are renowned for their intricate artwork and lively festivals, and the Santhals of eastern India are recognized for their strong sense of community and historical resistance to oppression.

These examples highlight the diversity of India's tribal cultures, each contributing its unique strengths to the nation's cultural mosaic. By appreciating and celebrating these traditions, society can foster greater unity and work toward a more just and equitable future.

Adivasis enjoy the unparalleled gift of living in nature, surrounded by unpolluted environments that foster collective happiness. Their communities are closely bonded, with a strong spirit of cooperation and mutual support, which enables them to live harmoniously rather than in competition with one another.

Around the globe, nations grapple with ecological challenges, prompting the establishment of legal frameworks to ensure environmental preservation. Many countries have implemented various schemes to contribute to global environmental protection. In India, the Constitution stands as the supreme law, incorporating several articles dedicated to environmental conservation. Notably, the 42nd Amendment in 1976 introduced two pivotal articles Article 48-A[154], emphasizing the protection, improvement, and preservation of forests and wildlife, and Article 51A (g)[155], underscoring the importance of environmental protection.

In the intricate web of global challenges, the nexus between environmental concerns and indigenous rights stands as a critical juncture demanding attention. As the world grapples with pressing issues related to climate change, biodiversity loss, and sustainable development, it is essential to recognize and address the unique relationship that indigenous communities have with their environments. This article explores the complex interplay

---

154. Constitution of India, Article 48A.
155. Constitution of India, Article 51-A(g).

between environmental concerns and indigenous rights, shedding light on the significance of navigating this intersection for the well-being of both the planet and its original inhabitants.

India, renowned for its ancient civilization, has witnessed the transformation of civilizations over time. While historical civilizations were inherently focused on the environment, the advent of modern industrialized and consumer-oriented societies has introduced new challenges, including environmental degradation and associated crimes. In response to these global challenges, international conventions and declarations have been established.

In the context of the nation-state governance system, the formulation and enactment of laws serve as effective tools for regulating human and market behavior. Various domestic laws have been enacted to address environmental concerns, with customary practices, legal customs, and scholarly writings collectively contributing to the evolution of global environmental law. This comprehensive legal framework seeks to address the issue of environmental crimes and their impact on individuals connected to these activities. In a detailed report, the growth of environmental crimes and their repercussions on affected communities is examined.

I. Indigenous People and their Inherent Connection with Environment

Indigenous communities worldwide have upheld a profound and longstanding connection with their ancestral lands. Their traditional wisdom, cultural rituals, and sustainable ways of life are intricately woven into the ecosystems they call home. The conservation of biodiversity, water sources, and natural scenery holds significance beyond ecological considerations for these communities; it is a fundamental aspect of cultural survival. Recognizing and honoring this intricate relationship is crucial for effectively tackling environmental challenges.

The term "environment" encompasses both the physical and biological aspects of our surroundings. It refers to the totality of circumstances in which we exist at any given moment or place. This comprehensive concept comprises interrelated biological, physical, and cultural systems that interact at both individual and group levels. An organism's habitat is formed by the collective conditions it must endure to sustain its life cycle, influencing the growth and development of living entities.

The environment plays a crucial role in the expansion and development of living things, encompassing various components essential for human well-being and the surroundings. Its functions are diverse and significant, including the provision of resources and raw materials for production. These resources, whether renewable or non-renewable, encompass items like land and wood for furniture.

Furthermore, the environment is vital for sustaining life by providing essential elements such as sun, soil, water, and air. These components are indispensable for human survival, contributing to genetic variation and supporting life processes. Additionally, the environment enhances the quality of life, as people derive appreciation from the beauty of nature, whether it is deserts, mountains, or rivers, thereby elevating the overall standard of living.

Indigenous groups, alternatively referred to as indigenous peoples, native peoples, or first peoples, are communities distinguished by their unique cultural, social, and historical identities. They typically represent the original inhabitants of a specific region or territory, having deep-rooted connections to their ancestral lands. Many indigenous groups have resided in these areas for generations, predating the arrival of colonizers, settlers, or other external groups. Indigenous communities are dispersed across the globe and are marked by their distinctive languages, traditions, customs, and frequently a profound spiritual or cultural affinity to the land.

II. Challenges Faced by Indigenous Communities

Despite the integral role indigenous community's play in environmental conservation, they often confront significant challenges related to environmental degradation. Encroachments on their lands, resource extraction, and the impacts of climate change disproportionately affect these communities, posing a direct threat to their traditional ways of life. Consequently, the struggle for indigenous rights becomes inseparable from the broader fight for environmental justice.

Indigenous communities are facing a multitude of difficulties to offenses, which worsen their existing vulnerabilities and jeopardize their way of life, cultural heritage and overall wellbeing. One major issue is the encroachment, on lands and resources through activities like land invasion, deforestation and illicit mining. These actions not harm. Reduce biodiversity but also violate indigenous land rights and hinder their ability to sustainably utilize natural resources based on their cultural traditions and ancestral knowledge[156].

Furthermore environmental crimes often lead to land, water and air pollution posing health hazards to groups who depend on these resources for their survival. Contamination from mining operations toxic waste disposal and industrial practices can result in health ailments such as respiratory diseases, waterborne illnesses and reproductive health challenges particularly impacting indigenous communities living near these polluted areas.

Moreover environmental offenses contribute to the decline of livelihoods and economic prospects for populations since unlawful exploitation of resources disrupts ecosystems exhausts natural reserves and undermines sustainable activities, like fishing, hunting and farming. This loss of livelihoods exacerbates poverty levels and food insecurity among groups leading to marginalization and weakening socio economic resilience.

Moreover environmental offenses often lead to conflicts and violence, within territories. Actions such as land seizure, deforestation and wildlife trafficking contribute to tensions and disagreements regarding land ownership, resource utilization and territorial control. Indigenous leaders and activists who oppose crimes frequently face threats, harassment and physical harm creating an atmosphere of fear and uncertainty in communities.

In essence environmental wrongdoing presents obstacles to the rights, livelihoods and welfare of groups. This perpetuates cycles of poverty, inequality and exclusion. Resolving these issues necessitates endeavors to bolster safeguards for indigenous land rights strengthen the enforcement of environmental regulations endorse community driven conservation projects

---

156. The Inconvenient Indian: A Curious Account of Native People in North America" by Thomas King

and encourage inclusive approaches to natural resource management that honor indigenous traditions and sovereignty. By acknowledging and responding to the vulnerabilities and requirements of populations stakeholders can strive for a fairer and more sustainable future, for everyone[157].

Environmental Crimes are covers a wide range of illicit activities that have detrimental effects on the environment, leading to significant ecological, social, and economic consequences. Those responsible for these offenses may be individuals, corporations, or governmental entities, and their actions often involve violations of environmental laws, regulations, and international agreements. Environmental crimes manifest in various ways, including[158]:

a) **Unlawful Timber Activities**: Unlawful timber activities encompass various illicit practices associated with logging and timber trade, often resulting in environmental degradation and social injustice. These activities include illegal logging, where timber is harvested in violation of national laws and regulations, leading to deforestation and biodiversity loss. Additionally, the laundering of illegally sourced timber through fraudulent documentation and misrepresentation in the supply chain is a prevalent form of unlawful activity. These practices contribute to the depletion of forest resources, disrupt ecosystems, and infringe upon the rights of indigenous communities, potentially leading to displacement and loss of livelihoods. Addressing unlawful timber activities requires robust enforcement, international cooperation, and the promotion of responsible practices throughout the timber supply chain to overcome the significant challenge they pose to sustainable forestry management.

b) **Unauthorized Fishing**: Unauthorized fishing refers to the practice of fishing activities conducted without proper legal authorization or in violation of established regulations. This phenomenon has significant and often detrimental effects on indigenous populations, particularly

---

157. Rebecca Tsossie- Indigenous People and Environmental Justice: The Impact of Climate Change

158. Indigenous Peoples Right, Amnesty International

those whose livelihoods and cultural identities are intricately linked to their local aquatic ecosystems.

Indigenous communities often rely on fishing as a primary source of sustenance, economic activity, and cultural heritage. Unauthorized fishing disrupts the delicate balance of aquatic environments, leading to overexploitation of fish stocks and depletion of crucial marine resources. This has direct consequences on the availability of traditional food sources for indigenous populations, threatening their food security and nutritional well-being.

Furthermore, the environmental impact of unauthorized fishing extends beyond resource depletion. Destructive fishing practices, such as the use of illegal gear or techniques, can harm the overall health of marine ecosystems. Indigenous communities, whose identities are often deeply rooted in a harmonious relationship with nature, experience cultural erosion as their traditional practices become unsustainable due to external pressures.

Moreover, unauthorized fishing exacerbates existing power imbalances, as indigenous populations often lack the resources and legal mechanisms to protect their fishing grounds. This can lead to conflicts over access to and control of marine resources, further marginalizing indigenous communities and undermining their ability to exercise their rights over ancestral lands.

In essence, unauthorized fishing poses a multifaceted threat to the well-being of indigenous populations, affecting not only their economic stability but also their cultural integrity and broader ecological sustainability. Addressing this issue requires a comprehensive approach that combines legal enforcement, community empowerment, and international collaboration to ensure the protection of both marine ecosystems and the rights of indigenous peoples.

c) **Wildlife Poaching:** Wildlife poaching, the illegal hunting or capturing of wild animals has far-reaching consequences that extend beyond the targeted species, impacting ecosystems and, notably, indigenous communities. Indigenous people often depend on their natural surroundings for sustenance, cultural practices, and spiritual beliefs. The effects of wildlife poaching on indigenous communities are manifold. Firstly, the depletion of key animal species disrupts the delicate balance of ecosystems, affecting the availability of resources crucial for indigenous livelihoods. Many indigenous communities rely on wildlife for food, medicine, and materials for cultural practices, making the loss of these species a direct threatto their traditional way of life.

Secondly, the increased demand for wildlife products in illegal markets can escalate tensions between indigenous communities and poachers, leading to conflicts over resources and territorial disputes. This not only jeopardizes the safety of indigenous people but also exacerbates existing challenges related to land rights and encroachment on their territories.

Additionally, the economic consequences of wildlife poaching can further marginalize indigenous communities. As valuable species decline due to poaching, the economic opportunities associated with sustainable resource management, ecotourism, and traditional practices diminish, leaving indigenous populations vulnerable to poverty and exploitation.

In summary, wildlife poaching poses a multifaceted threat to indigenous people, impacting their cultural heritage, food security, and overall well-being. Efforts to combat poaching must prioritize the inclusion of indigenous perspectives, acknowledging their role as stewards of the environment and empowering them in the conservation of biodiversity.

d) **Improper Waste Disposal:** Improper waste disposal poses a grave threat to the well-being of indigenous communities and their environments. Indigenous people often inhabit ecologically sensitive areas, relying on the land and its resources for their cultural practices and sustenance. When waste is improperly disposed of, contaminating water sources, soil, and air, it directly jeopardizes the health of these communities. The toxic substances from improper waste disposal can infiltrate traditional hunting and fishing grounds, leading to the bioaccumulation of harmful pollutants in the flora and fauna that indigenous people depend on for their diet. Additionally, the proximity of many indigenous communities to waste disposal sites exposes them to heightened health risks, as pollutants can enter their living spaces, causing respiratory problems and other health issues. The adverse effects of improper waste disposal exacerbate the challenges faced by indigenous peoples, further underscoring the importance of sustainable waste management practices to preserve both their cultural heritage and the integrity of their environments.

i. Air Quality Issues; when communities, in regions affected by air quality like from factories or wildfires experience respiratory problems and health issues. Their way of life which revolves around nature and natural resources gets disrupted, impacting their mental health.

ii. Water Pollution Concerns; The pollution of water sources due to activities or waste disposal poses a danger to groups access to clean water. This not impacts their health. Also disrupts cultural practices like fishing and spiritual rituals that rely on water bodies.

iii. Wildlife Trafficking; Indigenous peoples depend on wildlife for food, culture and livelihood. Illegal wildlife trade threatens these resources and traditional hunting practices. This loss of biodiversity endangers food sources. Weakens ties, to the land.

iv. Harmful Fishing Practices; Cyanide fishing used for capturing reef fish harms marine ecosystems and native fishing communities.

v. Indigenous fisher folk who rely on reefs, for their livelihoods face impacts due to the decline in fish populations, destruction of coral habitats and pollution of marine environments from cyanide fishing activities.

vi. Unregulated Fishing Practices; Indigenous fishing communities typically use fishing methods and sustainable resource management systems to support their way of life and protect biodiversity. However uncontrolled fishing practices like blast fishing and bottom trawling put these communities at risk by reducing fish stocks harming habitats and challenging traditional fishing customs.

In conclusion environmental offenses such as breaches in air quality standards, pollution of water sources illicit wildlife trade, cyanide fishing and unregulated fishing methods present obstacles to the health, livelihoods and cultural heritage of peoples. Addressing these issues necessitates efforts to enhance safeguards for indigenous rights uphold environmental regulations advocate for sustainable resource management approaches and encourage meaningful engagement with indigenous communities, in decisions affecting their lands and wellbeing.

Addressing the intricate challenge of combating environmental criminality while safeguarding the rights of indigenous people involves several recommendations;

i.   **Community-Led Conservation Efforts**: A promising approach to address the intersection of environmental concerns and indigenous rights involves promoting community-led conservation initiatives. Indigenous communities, armed with traditional knowledge and sustainable practices, frequently spearhead successful conservation efforts. Empowering these communities to actively manage their natural resources fosters a holistic approach that simultaneously benefits the environment and enhances indigenous well-being.

ii. **Partnerships and Collaborations**: Effectively navigating the intersection of environmental and indigenous concerns necessitates collaborative efforts involving governments, non-governmental organizations, and indigenous communities. Establishing partnerships that respect indigenous rights and integrate traditional ecological knowledge can lead to innovative solutions for environmental challenges. Recognizing the importance of inclusive dialogue, mutual respect, and cultural sensitivity is crucial in building successful collaborations.

iii. **Enhancing Legal Protections**: Enhance and enforce environmental laws to ensure robust protection for the vital natural resources and ecosystems essential to the well-being of indigenous communities, Implement and strengthen legal mechanisms dedicated to addressing and penalizing environmental crimes that directly impact indigenous lands.

Respecting and Acknowledging Indigenous Rights: Uphold the rights of indigenous populations as enshrined in international agreements such as the United Nations Declaration on the Rights of Indigenous Peoples (UNDRIP).[159] Ensure that indigenous groups are granted the fundamental right of free, prior, and informed consent (FPIC) in all decisions related to land use, resource management, and other activities affecting their territories.[160]

Promoting Sustainable Practices: Advocate for the widespread adoption of sustainable resource management practices that align with the ecological wisdom and traditional knowledge of indigenous societies. Encourage the integration of indigenous perspectives into broader conservation and sustainability initiatives, recognizing their unique contributions to environmental stewardship.

These measures collectively contribute to a comprehensive approach aimed at protecting boththe environment and the rights of indigenous communities. They emphasize the importance of legal frameworks, respect for indigenous rights, and the promotion of sustainable practices to address the complex challenges at the intersection of environmental conservation and indigenous well-being.

---

159. United Nations Declaration on the Rights of Indigenous Peoples (UNDRIP), United Nations General Assembly, 2007.

160. Office of the United Nations High Commissioner for Human Rights (OHCHR). *Report on the Rights of Indigenous Peoples* (2013).

Chapter 12
Judicial Contributions

By upholding the constitutional right to a clean and healthy environment, the Indian judiciary has in fact made a tremendous contribution to preserving and protecting the environment. The basic right to life has been expanded by the Supreme Court and High Courts in a number of major decisions, which have been interpreted as a right to live with dignity that includes the right to a clean environment.

The Indian judicial system has also taken the initiative to address environmental problems and has fought for environmental justice. It has frequently adopted an active stance, urging the government and other authorities to take action to save the environment and promote sustainable development.

Moreover, the Indian Judiciary has kept pace with the ever-evolving and changing landscape of technology and diverse fields, including environmental sciences. Its decisions have been instrumental in shaping Indian environmental law and have provided a framework for the development of comprehensive and dynamic environmental legislation.

The Indian Judiciary's contribution to environmental protection and conservation is not limited to the Indian subcontinent. It has been recognized globally for its role in shaping the environmental jurisprudence and has been a source of inspiration for other countries, both developed and developing.

Judicial independence is guaranteed by the Indian Constitution, which ensures that the judiciary is separate from both the legislative and executive arms of government. As a result, the Judiciary is better equipped to balance the demands of development projects against people' basic right to a clean and healthy environment, resisting pressure from both branches and remaining steadfast in opposition to executive measures.

The Supreme Court of India has adopted the principle of sustainable development, acknowledging that development is necessary for economic growth but also causes pollution. The Indian judiciary has played a crucial role in promoting sustainable development while reducing environmental harm.

The concept of environmental obligations is addressed in Part IV-A of the Indian Constitution, titled "Fundamental Duties," and Article 51-A(g) outlines citizens' responsibility to maintain and develop a healthy environment. Great environmental lawyers, such as Sh. M.C Mehta and Hon'ble Justice Kuldeep Singh, have contributed significantly to the development of Indian environmental law.

The courts have the power to intervene when obligations are neglected, and citizens' right to life is at risk. The court has ruled that it is the state's and citizens' duty to protect and improve the environment, forests, rivers, lakes, and animals, and that the principles of rights and responsibilities are interconnected.

The judiciary has played a crucial role in protecting the environment in India. Some of the notable cases and actions taken by the judiciary in this regard are:

1. The Supreme Court of India, in the case of *"M.C. Mehta v. Union of India (1987)"*[161], ordered the closure of industries in Delhi that were polluting the air and water. This led to the establishment of the Delhi Pollution Control Committee and the improvement of air and water quality in the city.

2. In the case of *"Vellore Citizens Welfare Forum v. Union of India (1996)"*,[162] the Supreme Court issued directions to the Tamil Nadu Pollution Control Board to take action against polluting industries in the state. The court also held that the polluter pays principle should

---

161. AIR 1987 SC 965

162. AIR 1996 SC 2715

be applied, and industries should compensate for the damage caused to the environment.

3. The Supreme Court, in the case of "***Subhash Kumar v. State of Bihar (1991)***[163]", held that the right to life includes the right to a clean environment. This judgment has been cited in many subsequent cases related to environmental protection.

4. In the case of "***Rural Litigation and Entitlement Kendra v. State of Uttar Pradesh (1985)***[164]", the Supreme Court ordered the closure of limestone quarries in the Dehradun-Mussoorie region of Uttarakhand, which were causing environmental damage.

5. In the case of "***T.N. Godavarman Thirumulpad v. Union of India (1996)***[165]", the Supreme Court issued directions to protect forests across the country. The court also appointed a Central Empowered Committee to monitor the implementation of its orders.

Overall, the judiciary has been proactive in protecting the environment in India. The courts have issued orders and directives to control pollution, protect forests, and safeguard the right to a clean environment. The judiciary has also played a crucial role in enforcing environmental laws and holding polluters accountable.

The judiciary is critical to environmental preservation. Here are some of the landmark environmental judgements:

I. "*Vellore Citizens Welfare Forum

V.

Union of India, 1996 5 SCR 241[166]

Appellant - Vellore Citizens Welfare Forums.

---

163. AIR 1991 SC 420
164. AIR 1985 SC 652
165. (1997) 2 SCC 267
166. 1996 5 SCR 241

Respondent: The Secretary of the Union of India, Department of Environment, and others

Justices- Justice Kuldip Singh, Faizan Uddin J., and K. Venkataswami J.,

Judgment was given by - Supreme Court

Judgment was given on: April 7, 2016.

Facts

The case has been given a principle *"the Precautionary Principle"* which plays a vital feature in "Sustainable Development".

The precautionary principles give decision-makers the authority to take preventive measures, when there is doubt regarding the scientific findings, regarding harm environment or human health and the stakes are high.

Vellore Citizens Welfare Forum, the petitioner in this case, acted in line with Article 32 of the Constitution. The river Palar in the State of Tamil Nadu was seriously polluted by tanneries and other enterprises, which is why the appeal was filed. The Palar River served as the region's primary supply of water for people' daily needs. Later, it was revealed by the Vellore-based Tamil Nadu Agricultural University Research Centre that some 35,000 hectares of agricultural land had turned completely or partially barren and was no longer suitable for farming. In one of its important rulings, the Supreme Court gave great thought to the linkages between economic growth and the environment.

Issues

- Should the tanneries be allowed to continue working at a cost to humans and wellness of the environment?

  Arguments are given by the Petitioner and the Respondent-

Petitioner

The petitioner's knowledgeable attorney said that the river Palar's whole surface and groundwater supply had been contaminated, rendering it unfit for human consumption. They continued by saying that the tanneries in Tamil Nadu had seriously harmed the environment in the area. An assessment of 13 towns in the Dindigul and Peddiar Chatram Panchayat Unions by a non-administrative organization revealed that 350 of the 467 wells used for drinking water and water system purposes were found to be contaminated.

Respondent

Supporters of the tanneries argued that the Board's (TDS) quality standards were invalid. This Court requested the NEERI to do a study on the subject and offer its conclusion in an order dated April 9, 1996. In its report, NEERI validated the models the Board had suggested. The Ministry of Environment and Forests has not yet finished developing total dissolved solids, sulphate, and chloride discharge models for inland and surface water. Each State Pollution Control Board makes the call regarding these restrictions based on the specifications backed by regional site conditions. It is been advised that you adhere to the rules set forth by the (TNPCB).

Judgment

The Apex Court made the decision to make every effort to maintain harmony between the environment and growth after hearing from all parties and reviewing the evidence. The Court emphasised that these tanneries are the main source of foreign currency for the nation and that they also give a lot of people work. But it also puts everyone's health and the ecology at danger. A court ruling that granted the petitioners' request mandates that all tanneries pay a fee of Rs. 10,000 by depositing the money at the Collector's office. The Court further ordered Tamil Nadu to pay Mr. M. C. Mehta Rs. 50,000 as compensation for his efforts to save the environment.

II. "*INDIAN ENVIRO LEGAL COUNSEL*

V.

***UNION OF INDIA and OTHERS, 1996 AIR 1446*[167]**

Case Citation - 1996 AIR 1446, 1996 SCC (3) 212,

---

167. 1996 AIR 1446

Dated – 13th February 1996,

Petitioner in the case- Indian Council for Enviro Legal Action,

Respondents- UOI and others,

Judges- Justice B.P. Jeevan Reddy and Justice B.N. Kripal,

Statutes- Implementation of the *"polluter pays principle"* for the first time.

The widely accepted *"polluter pays"* principle states that those responsible for pollution ought to take steps to reduce it to protect the environment and well-being of humans.

Facts

In this case, a writ application was made by a group named the Indian Council for Environmental Legal Action. This organisation expressed worry over a small hamlet called Bichhri village in the Udaipur region of Rajasthan. Chemical industrial businesses including Hindustan Zinc Ltd. and countless others were located in this village's northern area. The main worry was how entrepreneurs in the buggy sector would use these chances to boost their profit margins through exports and the encouragement of industrialisation.

The fourth responder, Hindustan Agro Chemicals, started producing concentrated sulfuric acid, often known as oleum, and a single super phosphate in 1987. At the time, it was believed that these items posed a major threat to those living in the nearby communities. Following this, TataSilver Chemicals, the fifth responder, started producing "H" acid as well and gave me the identical complex. The bulk of acid H was produced for the export market. The second responder, Jyoti Compounds, arrived from a separate compound that mostly produced "H" acids as well as a variety of other dangerous substances.

To produce fertilizers and other chemicals that in some way or another contributed to environmental damage, numerous more chemical enterprises were also set up. In this instance, all of the respondents were discharging hazardous waste in this particular area of Bichhri village, which was not even receiving adequate care from these industrial facilities. Water, air, soil, and anything else that came in connection with these industrial effluents were all polluted and unfit for use by humans or animals.

Three hundred seventy-five tonnes of acid "H" and a total of 2500 tonnes of highly atomic waste were also generated; both of these products were destined for export. The report that was filed had this information. These dangerous compounds all impacted soil, groundwater, and contributed to the contamination of water streams. Over time, these dangerous substances substantially polluted the water and made it unsafe for ingestion. Many inhabitants used these water streams for drinking, irrigation, and soil fertilisation as their primary source of subsistence. The pollution also contributed to a number of diseases, issues, and fatalities in the adjacent communities.

The parliament raised concern about the abrupt worsening, the administration vowed that proper action would be taken, but nothing was done. As a result, there was a virtual uprising among the locals, and the DM finally utilised section 144 of the CrPC to order the closure of these enterprises.

Issues in case

1. Is the respondent obligated to pay the quantity necessary to carry out the rightful action?

2. Did the companies that make these dangerous compounds have implemented any environmental safeguards?

Petitioner's Argument

The petitioners' opening statement focused on the fact that the defendant industries began producing "H" acid and other chemicals in a facility that was part of a larger complex in the Bichhri village. The production significant amount of toxic waste from industry, particularly iron-based and gypsum-based effluent, primarily aids a generation of sludge that was never effectively treated by safety standards. As a result, it was demanded that the plants be shut down immediately. To protect the environment and its resources, manufacturing should also be put on hold until the waste is properly managed.

Additionally, the petitioner stated, nearly all respondent industries had requested a "NOC" from the government for the manufacturing of these dangerous chemicals, which clearly shows that doing so will result in significant environmental destruction.

Defendant's Argument

The defendant countered and submitted a counter affidavit in support of their claims. They made the following claims in their assertion: Hindustan Agro Chemicals Limited: In accordance with their affidavits, the Pollution Control Board had previously granted this plant a "NOC" for the production of sulphuric acid and alumina sulphate, subject to several strict compliance requirements under the Water [Pollution Prevention and Control] Act of 1974, and the Air (Pollution Prevention and Control Act) Act of 1981. After that, they began to produce oleum and single super phosphate (S.S.P.), but they also noted that many of the dangerous substances found are resistant, making treatment difficult.

The Principle Applied

The "Polluter Pay Principle," which mandates that the polluter pay for all expenditures incurred as part of the charges for pollution, was cited by the court.

This theory was developed in response to the ongoing debate over "absolute liability" in the case of M.C. Mehta v. Union of India, where the court ordered that those who cause pollution must pay a fine that will be used to improve living and environmental conditions for those who live in the affected regions.

This principle was also governed by Articles 48-A and 51-A(g) of the Indian Constitution in the case of Vellore Citizens Welfare Forum v. Union of India and others, and the principle can be derived from existing legislation. Even though the corporation in the Oleum Gas Leak case complied with all applicable rules, including the Air Act of 1981, the Apex Court found Shriram Factories accountable for the Oleum gas leak and the environmental impact.

The question of whether the polluter should just be sued civilly or if criminal charges against the polluters are also necessary are still up for debate. The protection of the rights to community participation, life, and personal liberty is guaranteed by Article 21 of the Constitution, and environmental preservation inevitably follows.

Decision made by the court

This principle was also governed by Articles 48-A and 51-A(g) of the Indian Constitution in the case of Vellore Citizens Welfare Forum v. Union of India and others, and the principle can be derived from existing legislation. Even though the corporation in the Oleum Gas Leak case complied with all applicable rules, including the Air Act of 1981, the Apex Court found Shriram Factories accountable for the Oleum gas leak and the environmental impact.

The question of whether the polluter should just be sued civilly or if criminal charges against the polluters are also necessary are still up for debate. The protection of the rights to community participation, life, and personal liberty is guaranteed by Article 21 of the Constitution, and environmental preservation inevitably follows.

The respondent industries would be responsible for paying INR 37,385,000 in addition to 12% compound interest yearly if the money wasn't paid in full or made up for by April 11, 1997. The respondent industries were also ordered to cover the costs of the action because they willfully wasted the court's time and resources. Following the court's ruling, the lawsuit was obliged to continue for a further 15 years, during which petitioners were required to maintain their position. The court directed the respondent industries to pay a sum of Rs. 10,000 INR as costs in regard to both interlocutory petitions after taking into account all relevant facts and inferences from the case.

In addition to this, the amount of money will be utilized, as directed by relevant authorities, to carry out necessary actions in and around the Rajasthani village of Bichhri and its surrounding areas.

As a result, the court utilised it for the first time. the ***"Polluter Pays Principle,"*** requiring all major industrialists to compensate for endangering the environment and putting a threat to villagers' lives by failing to properly dispose of their plants' hazardous waste.

III. *"RURAL LITIGATION and ENTITLEMENT KENDRA and OTHERS*

V.

STATE OF UTTAR PRADESH, AIR 1985 S.C. 652[168]

Case Title - Rural Litigation and Entitlement Kendra and Others v/s State of Uttar Pradesh, 1985

Citation of the case - AIR 1985 S.C. 652, 1985 SCR (3) 169,

Appellant- Rural Litigation and Entitlement Kendra,

Respondent - State of UP,

Judges - J. P.N. Bhagwati, J. Amerendra Nath and Justice Rangnath Mishra.

Facts

The Himalayan hill range near Mussoorie includes Doon Valley. The Doon Valley region had great prosperity. The Mussoorie hills are the source of several rivers, which has helped the ecological success of the valley area. But in the 1950s, it became a district for limestone mines, and the valley began to deteriorate as a result of the extensive mining, use of explosives, and tree-cutting.

Between 1955 and 1965, the Doon Valley saw large limestone mining activities. The usage of detonating to extract minerals was the reason why there was no flora in the valley. By the early 1980s, landslides, floods, water shortages, intense heat, and the devastation of crops had taken the majority of the valley's natural beauty away.

In 1961, the mining sector was made illegal by the state of Uttar Pradesh's minister of mines. However, quarrying began in 1962 after the state's administration settled on a number of mining leases lasting about 20 years.

---

168. AIR 1985 S.C. 652

In 1982, the states outlawed leases for regeneration because of the harm they would do to the environment. The rulings of the government were challenged in court by mining businesses. The Allahabad High Court approved the Doon Valley mining project, prioritising financial gain over environmental concerns.

In 1983, the (RLEK), a small Dehradun-based NGO, filed a suit with the Supreme Court of India about environmental poverty. According to Article 32 of the Constitution, this issue was brought before the Apex Court as a writ petition. The Apex Court mandates an examination of all ongoing mining activities in the valley. The state's creation of a database for the local agriculture sector was another topic the court emphasised.

Issues raised in the case

In this particular instance, the following questions were examined by the Honorable Supreme Court:

1. Whether or the Forest Conservation Act of 1980, would apply to the lease renewal process? In 1962, mining operations granted leases, and in 1980, a forest protection act was established.

2. Whether mining operations in government forests violated the Forest Conservation Act. Non-forest actions on forest land that are not authorized by the national government are forbidden by the legislation.

3. Should national economic help take precedence over environmental conservation?

The Petitioner's argument

- Doon Valley residents' ability to live their daily lives will be hindered by environmental devastation, which violates their fundamental right to a nourishing environment. The right to have a healthy environment is a part of the right to life, according to Article 21 of the Constitution.

- The public's rejection of lease restitution caused the state to withdraw its approval for mining.

- As forests are listed as coexisting resources, extraction activities ought to require national government approval.

The Respondent's argument

- The state's administrative authorities acting under the Environmental Protection Act should be informed of the problematic situation, not the Supreme Court. Whether the state should have jurisdiction over the Respondents' assertion that the Mines Act of 1952's restrictions applied to all mining and quarrying practises.

- The continuation of mining operations is necessary for the protection of the country's foreign exchange location and should not be stopped.

- Mine workers and other labourers will lose their jobs if mining is stopped.

Observations

Procedures have continued since the Supreme Court considered the case in 1983. While this issue was still proceeding in court, the Parliament passed the Environment Protection Act in 1980. The respondent council claims that the new legislation satisfies the necessary requirements, and that the court should thus dismiss the action. The matter should be handled by the body in charge of enforcing the EPA Act, not by the court. The claim was denied by the court since the litigation had already started and significant testaments, evidence, and other instructions had been given before the legislation was established.

Respondents said that when undertaking mining operations, they complied with the relevant laws including the 1952 Mining Act. The Bhargava committee was established by the court to clarify the situation. Based on the Bhargava committee's findings, the court determined that the most dangerous mines in Mussoorie City should be shut down. The court assigned the Bandyopadhyay Committee, the second committee, the job of examining the first committee's findings in 1985. This group also recommended aiding the valley's underprivileged citizens. After learning about the valley's environmental impoverishment, the court awarded many mining corporations licences to operate there. Because the environmental impact was less obvious, a sizable enterprise controlled by the state of Uttar Pradesh could be able to continue.

The decision by Court

At the same time the Supreme Court took up the matter, the Central Government started to worry about the crucial mining activities in the Valley. The Indian government provided a working group with the limestone investigation for the Dehradun-Mussoorie region in 1983 as part of the Dehradun Valley Litigation case. The government Working Group and the court's committee reached the same conclusions on the mines' detrimental effects on the environment, according to the same individual, D.N. Bhargava. Additionally, the Working Group created reports on the limited mining enterprises that were still allowed to operate for the court. While the matter was being heard in court, the Environment Protection Act was passed by Parliament in 1986.

IV. "SUBHASH KUMAR

V.

STATE OF BIHAR and OTHERS, AIR 1991 SC 420[169]

Citation of the case - AIR 1991 SC 420,

Petitioner - Subhash Kumar,

Respondents - State of Bihar and others

Benches - Justice K. N. Singh and Justice N. D. Ojha,

Facts of the case

The Supreme Court was petitioned by Subhash Kumar to force Tata Iron and Steel Co. mills that discharge slurry to cease polluting the Bokaro River. The petitioner claims that the defendants disregarded Section 24 of the Water (Prevention and Control of Pollution Act, 1978), which prohibits the discharge of hazardous or polluting materials into rivers, and that they also failed to

---

169. AIR 1991 SC 420

maintain the quality of the water. The State Pollution Control Board was established to carry out the duties outlined in Sec. 17 of the aforementioned Act. The Board is recommended to review data and standards related to water treatment, sewage treatment facilities, and commercial effluents.

The West Bokaro Collieries, commonly known as the Tata Iron and Steel Co., allegedly conducted mining operations in Jamshedpur, according to the petitioner (Subhash Kumar). According to the allegations, these mining operations discharge their waste as slurry, which gathers on the river's bed and starts to settle on surrounding land, including plot number 170, which belongs to the petitioner. He emphasized that the mining plant's discharge pollutes the water that is then used for irrigation or human or animal usage, and that the slurry settles on the agricultural soil, leaving a thin coating of carboniferous. As the State of Bihar is leasing land to various people in exchange for royalties paid for the collection of slurry, The State Pollution Control Board did not punish the corporation as required.

The petitioner demanded that the Tata Iron and Steel Co. face extrajudicial action under the relevant provisions of the Act, and that the defendants immediately take measures to prevent the discharge of slurry into the Bokaros River. However, the defence attorneys responded by filing counter-affidavits claiming that the petitioner had only filed the PIL to further his own interests rather than to protect the rights of the wider affected public. They stated that the petitioner had been purchasing slurry from the Tata Company for many years and only filed multiple lawsuits at the district and state levels after the company stopped doing business with him. When the lower courts did not rule in his favor, he then appealed to a higher court by submitting the same allegations in the form of a PIL.

Issues raised in the case

1. What the PIL is for—a matter of public or private interest?

2. Is the river Bokaro contaminated by the defendant's mining facility's discharge of slurry?

The argument presented by Plaintiff

The petitioner, Subhash Kumar, claimed that the slurry waste discharged by the Tata Iron and Steel Co. washers only slightly contaminates the water of the river Bokaro. He further claimed that the ongoing consumption of sludge presented serious health concerns to individuals and that water transported to rural areas was unsuitable for drinking or use in agriculture. Furthermore, it claimed that the Bihar government ignored repeated demands and even offered royalties in exchange for lease payments. In his appeal, he argued that the defendants—the state of Bihar and the Bihar Pollution Control Board— should get an order addressing the question of direction.

Arguments are given by Defendant

The Board has given Tata Iron and Steel Co. permission to discharge effluents from its outlets, according to the defendants, in accordance with Sections 25 and 26 of the Water Prevention and Control of Pollution Act, 1974. The Bihar Pollution Control Board investigated and evaluated all the information to demonstrate that the effluents produced by the washers during the mining activities did not contaminate the river before approving the release of the effluents to the Bokaro River. According to the respondents, the Board gave the Director of the Collieries instructions to enhance the river's condition in order to prevent pollution of the Bokaro River. The respondents said that four ponds were built to boost the effluents' storage capacity.

The defendants argued that there was no evidence of slurries being discharged into the river, and therefore, there was no concern about the river's contamination or the productivity of the land being affected. They also highlighted that the Bokaro River used to be dry for nine months, and the slurry that collected in the pond was considered valuable due to its carboniferous minerals, which made it useful as fuel. The Company had taken steps to prevent any slurry from leaking out of the pond because it was essential for fuel production. Given the high market value of slurry, the corporation could not afford to let it end up in the river. As a result, the Company had implemented all necessary safety measures to ensure that no slurry leaked into the pond.

RELATED PROVISIONS IN THE CASE

- Article 32 of the Indian Constitution of 1950 gives that the parliament of India may, by law, be granted permission by any other court to utilize all or some of the Supreme Court's authority within the sphere of its local jurisdiction. That allows individuals to seek redress when they feel that their rights have been "unduly deprived." As a result, we can conclude that this article provides persons with an assured right by giving them access to the Supreme Court and ensuring the protection of their basic rights.

- The Water Prevention and Control of Pollution Act of 1974 applies to the states of Jammu and Kashmir, Rajasthan, Kerala, West Bengal, Assam, Bihar, Madhya Pradesh, Gujarat, Haryana, Tripura, and the union territories. This law was put into place to stop and manage water contamination as well as to improve and sustain the establishment's access to clean water. To manage water body pollution, the Act also grants some authority to formed authorities like the central board and the state board immediately without first going through a more drawn-out procedure of going via lower courts.

- Under Article 226 of the Indian Constitution, which went into effect in 1950, High Courts can issue orders, writs, or directions to any person or authority, including the relevant government, to enforce any of the rights guaranteed by Part III and for "any other reason." the Supreme Court.

The court dismissed a public interest petition filed by the petitioner as it was found that the Board had taken effective measures to prevent factory waste from being dumped into the river. The court further ruled that to invoke the jurisdiction of the court under Article 32, it must be done to protect the fundamental rights of the parties concerned and not out of personal animosity or anger. The court recognized its responsibility to discourage such petitions and ensure that the course of justice is not complicated or tainted by litigants who file petitions under the guise of public interest litigation for personal matters.

The petitioner attempted to persuade the respondents to provide him with more slurry due to his strong business acumen and coal sales license.

When his requests were refused, he resorted to harassing them. The petitioner also filed several petitions in the Patna High Court under Article 226 of the Constitution, seeking permission to collect slurry from the raiyat land. The court rejected the plea and ordered the petitioner to pay the respondents 5,000 rupees, taking into account all available evidence.

V. *"MURLI S. DEORA*

V.

UNION OF INDIA 2001 8 SCC 765[170]

Case No - Writ Petition (Civil) 316 of 199

Petitioner: Murli S. Deora

Respondents - UOI and Ors.

Judgement Delivery: 02/11/2001

Benches: J. M.B. Shah and J. R.P Sethi.

Facts

Murli S. Deora submitted a civil writ suit in the Supreme Court of India in 1999 under Article 32 of the Constitution challenging the ban on smoking in public places. A two-judge panel made up of M. B. Shah and R. P. Sethi heard the plea.

In India, tobacco (cigarette) use is responsible for almost 800,000 deaths yearly. Injurious internal conditions like lung cancer, asthma, and chronic bronchitis can result from smoking in public places in front of non-smokers. Smoking in public spaces is therefore prohibited since it endangers the health of numerous passive smokers and violates their right to live a healthy life. In addition to having detrimental effects on health, it also harms the ecosystem. It causes environmental pollution and worsens the state of the ecological system.

---

170. 2001 8 SCC 765

Issues raised in the case

1. Whether smoking in public places infringes upon non-smokers' right as stated in Article 21 of the Constitution?

2. Whether it is necessary to outlaw smoking in public areas?

Arguments are given in the court

The petitioner argued that tobacco contains harmful substances such as nicotine, tar, potential carcinogens, carbon monoxide, irritants, and smoke particles that have been linked to several diseases, including cancer. According to the petitioner, three million people die each year from tobacco-related diseases, with one million of them residing in developing countries like India. The World Health Organization has estimated that tobacco use can lead to up to seven million deaths annually. The petitioner also argued that smoking causes air pollution. The petitioner pointed out that smoking bans are not included in the Cigarettes (Regulation of Production, Supply, and Distribution) Act 1975 or the Cigarettes and Other Products (Prohibition of Advertisement) Act. Therefore, the petitioner urged the court to prohibit smoking in public places in the interest of public health until regulatory rules are formulated and implemented.

In addition, the Attorney General and the respondents' attorney argued that smoking in public places must be prohibited due to the negative consequences of smoking.

Judgment

The Apex Court found, people who smoke in public places are violating the right to life of passive smokers. The Supreme Court issued an order banning smoking in public places after realizing the seriousness of the problem and the harm that smoking does to both smokers and passive smokers. Additionally, it gave the UOI, the State Governments, and the UT instructions to have the necessary ways to make sure that smoking is outlawed in public places like:-

- Auditoriums

- Hospitals and Health Institutions

- Educational Institutions

- Public Office and Court buildings.

VI. "SACHIDANANDA PANDEY

V

STATE OF WEST BENGAL and ORS, 1987[171] SCR (2) 223"

Petitioner - Indian Council for Environment Legal

Citation - AIR 1109, 1987 SCR (2) 223,

Judgement Delivery - 13 February 1996

Respondents - State of Bengal and Ors.

Bench - J. O. Chinnappa Reddy, J. V. Khalid.

Facts of the case

1. Also known as the "Town Planning Case", the facts of the suit is, the West Bengal government leases 4 acres of Calcutta Zoological Garden land to the Taj Group to build five-star hotels.

2. The Secretary of the Union of Workmen of the Zoological Garden and a live member of the zoo filed a PIL petition challenging the transfer of this 4-acre area to the Taj Company.

3. A lawsuit was filed in the Apex Court about the development of this hotel, which disturbed the animals of the zoo and disrupted the ecosystem of the surrounding flora, causing the plants to vanish as a result.

4. The Secretary stated that it disagreed with the idea of building a hotel on zoo property. The Committee objected in two ways:

---

171. 1987 SCR (2) 223

   A. The multi-story structure near the zoo will irritate animals, upset the ecological balance, and disrupt bird migration.

5. That site was already being utilized for a variety of things, including the cultivation of fodder, animal burial grounds, a hospital, an operating room, a nursery, a post-mortem room, and a quarantine section.

6. The Committee claims that it's not possible to fit the necessary works on the main zoo's ground place.

7. The allegations made by the Management Committee were first raised with the Minister for Metropolitan Development, who then wrote a letter to the Chief Minister underlining the same issue.

8. Following claims, the CM claimed, that the zoo required those amenities.

9. From that point on, the Management Committee changed its stance and agreed to the proposal on the confirmation that the zoo would get awards for the surrounding area and coordination with other organizations.

10. After that, the Management Board shifted its opinion and endorsed the proposal, confirming that the zoo would receive recognition for its cooperation with other associations and the surrounding region.

Issues in the case

1. Is there any chance that the respondent will cause ecological contamination?

2. Is the notion put out by the Local government Lawful?

Arguments are given by the Appellant

Under the watchful eye of the court, Dr L. M. Singhvi, a knowledgeable advisor, made the following entries for the advantage of the appellants: The Management Committee of the Zoological Garden had a legitimate ownership interest in the Begumbari Land. Also, it was argued that the Taj Group of Hotels shouldn't be permitted to lease the Land without first delivering a greeting para 166 and 167 of the Land Manual, according to their criteria, to the vulnerable volunteers. The decision was made by the authority without taking into account how it would affect the zoo negatively or without seeking the opinions of any other institutions or interested persons. Leading ornithologists nationwide, the director of the zoo, the zoo's management committee, the public undertakings committee of West Bengal, and the Indian Wildlife Board do not support the Taj Group of Hotels, and among others. These individuals and organizations offered several justifications for the unhappiness, but the government didn't take any of them into account. The Cabinet Memorandum ignored such objections; hence the government official did not take these protests into account. The learned counsel made the case that the government official made a poor decision since it was based solely on assumptions. Additionally, suspicions were formed without conducting the proper research and analysis. According to the appealing party, there is too much evidence of ecological catastrophe to even justify discounting it. In addition, the conditions hurt the government revenue used to pay land rent.

Arguments are given by the Defendant

However, Shri Dipankar Gupta, a learning guide for the Taj Group of Hotels, and Shri Gooptu learned guidance for the West Bengal state government, countered that the conclusion was meant to invigorate the travel industry while remaining neutral to any biological frameworks. Additionally, it takes into account the local environmental aspects of the area. The Stand is supported by the court in this instance, and respectable arbitrator Justice Chinnapa Reddy attested to it.

"Obviously if the government official is alert to the distinct thinking necessitating considerations and discussions that show up at the cognizant option after evaluating them, it may not be for this court to tamper without malice," remarked Justice Chinnapa Reddy.

Furthermore, it was argued that moving the burial ground and unloading area would make the area more sterile. It was made clear that there won't be any obstacles in the way of the meeting bird's journey because the lodging would be built 700 feet from the lake and rise to a maximum height of 75 feet, making it a medium ascent rather than an elevated structure. While the cargo dock, cemetery, and shabby buildings were to be replaced by a hotel surrounded by wide streets, it was also disputed that the area would have improved naturally as a result.

Judgment

The Honorable Supreme Court referenced the case of *"R.D. Shetty v. Global Airport Authority"*[172], in which the apex court decided that the government's actions had a public component, and that if it agreed, it ought to do it honourably, without stratification or needless effort. The government had to behave in accordance with values or requirements rather than acting arbitrarily, foolishly, or insignificantly. Whenever it handled people generally, whether by assigning positions, making agreements, granting portions or licences, or enabling various types of charges. In the unlikely event that the government deviated from such a norm or standard, regardless of the circumstances, its actions ran the risk of being invalidated, unless it could be demonstrated that the deviation was not self-aggrandizing but rather was based on a significant rule that wasn't absurd, silly, or oppressive.

So, the court was satisfied that the State of West Bengal acted completely honestly while renting out after taking into account the numerous facts and circumstances of the case, Begumbari land was granted to the Taj Group of Hotels for the construction of a five-star hotel in Calcutta. The West Bengal government did not ignore any pertinent considerations.

This manner, rather than inviting tenders or making a public sale, direct agreement with those who approached with recommendations to create Five Star Hotels was without a doubt the sanest and most impartial way to go with the subject. Since no other driving hotelier demonstrated any propensity to approach, the tactic adopted wasn't unjust. It was a proposal for government property. As a result, open closeout was essentially prohibited. The Taj Group of Hotels came out with a suggestion to start the hotel.

Natural justice principles impart key guidelines for choosing the government's exemplary behaviour. Its two main components are the right to a fair hearing and ruling against predilection. The court fairly observed that

---

172. AIR 1979 SC 1628

Natural Justice Requirements had been considered and those who are typically supportive of that Zoological Garden had been given a chance to be heard before a decision was made. The idea to lease the Begumbari was known to the general population. The Director of the Zoo and the members of the Management Committee of the Zoological Garden both voiced their opinions on the subject. In its report, the Public Undertakings Committee discussed the issue and praised the Government for its consideration of several factors. The issue was also discussed on the Legislative Assembly floor. Hence, it was challenging to agree that natural justice requirements had gone unnoticed.

Also, it was widely observed that the government was aware of the ideas put out by the boards of trustees and intrigued well beings. For instance, the open endeavour council's report was taken seriously since it stated that the construction of a five-star hotel nearby would negatively impact the migratory birds and reduce the ability of the zoo to rear its animal population. The purpose of the development, as stated by the Management Board of the Zoo, was to remove the feed development site and, as a result, probably definitely relocate the offices in that area to the Zoo's grounds. The Chief Minister of West Bengal assured them that the public authority will provide whatever additional offices they might need. Additionally, the rent was the culmination of a protracted, complex, and transparent process with nothing to hide, making it impossible to rationally rely on adversarial analysis.

In addition, the Government of West Bengal and the Taj group prioritised the travel of migratory birds, thus even though the area had a few high rises in the past, the design of the development was to limit height to no more than 75 feet. Throughout the birds' journey, it was never truly liberated. Additionally, due to a valid worry for the birds, it was agreed to reduce lighting within the hotel while maintaining the environmental features of the establishment and the surrounding flora.

Every single piece of data made it quite evident that the Taj group had provided all of the assurances required to save the Zoo and its prisoners. It has also been agreed that a new activity theatre, mortuary, veterinary division, and other facilities will be created for Rs. 30 lakhs, which the Taj family was eligible to receive under rent provision 25 but purposefully withheld.

The court was also informed that approximately 30000 plants were getting ready to beautify the development's exterior.

There was no doubt, then, that the public authority didn't give natural justice principles, environmental concerns, or migratory birds any prior consideration.

Here's a summary of the selected cases related to environmental law and environmental crime from 2020 and 2021-

1. Indian Council for Enviro-Legal Action v. Union of India, (2020) 10 SCC 1:

   - The Supreme Court addressed the pollution caused by industrial units and the need for stricter enforcement of environmental regulations. The court emphasized the responsibility of industries to adhere to pollution control norms.

2. State of Uttarakhand v. Jagat Ram, (2020) 4 SCC 587:

   - This case involved illegal mining activities in the state, leading to environmental degradation. The court upheld the ban on illegal mining and mandated strict penalties for offenders.

3. Sambhaji v. State of Maharashtra, 2020 SCC OnLine Bom 1201:

   - The Bombay High Court ruled on the illegal construction activities affecting ecologically sensitive areas, reinforcing the need for adherence to environmental clearance processes.

4. Mohammad Hadi v. State of Gujarat, 2020 SCC OnLine Guj 806:

   - The court examined the illegal trade in wildlife and emphasized the importance of protecting endangered species under the Wildlife Protection Act.

5. Sukhwinder Singh v. State of Punjab, (2020) 5 SCC 350:

   - This case dealt with pollution caused by brick kilns. The court ordered the closure of non-compliant units and highlighted the health impacts on local communities.

6. Prakash v. State of Himachal Pradesh, 2021 SCC OnLine HP 483:

    - The court addressed illegal construction in forest areas, emphasizing the need for compliance with the Forest Conservation Act.

7. Goa Foundation v. State of Goa, (2020) 5 Goa L.R. 267:

    - This case focused on illegal mining activities in Goa. The court ruled against the continuation of mining operations that posed significant environmental risks.

8. Shiv Shakti Co-operative Housing Society v. State of Maharashtra, (2020) 8 SCC 145:

    - The court dealt with the issue of unauthorized construction impacting mangroves and coastal ecosystems, mandating restoration efforts.

9. Bhim Singh v. State of Uttarakhand, 2020 SCC OnLine Utt 1184:

    - This case highlighted the illegal disposal of hazardous waste and the government's obligation to enforce waste management regulations.

10. M.C. Mehta v. Union of India, (2020) 5 SCC 451:

    - The Supreme Court reiterated the need for air quality management in Delhi, imposing measures to curb pollution levels.

11. Karnataka State Pollution Control Board v. Bhima Cements Ltd., 2020 SCC OnLine Kar 1966:

    - The court ruled on compliance with pollution control norms for cement manufacturing, stressing accountability for environmental harm.

12. **Vellore Citizens Welfare Forum v. State of Tamil Nadu**, 2020 SCC OnLine Mad 15455:

    - The judgment reinforced the principles of sustainable development and the precautionary principle in the context of industrial projects.

13. Environmental Action Group v. Union of India, (2021) 4 SCC 191:

    - The case discussed the regulatory framework for managing environmental assessments, emphasizing transparency and public participation.

14. Laxmi Narayan v. State of Rajasthan, (2021) 4 SCC 111:

   - The court ruled on the enforcement of water pollution standards in industrial operations, underlining the right to clean water.

15. Pradeep Singh v. State of Jharkhand, 2021 SCC OnLine Jhar 68:

   - The judgment addressed illegal mining and the necessity of comprehensive environmental assessments before granting mining licenses.

16. State of Kerala v. A.P. Raveendran, 2021 SCC OnLine Ker 2118:

   - The court emphasized the importance of preserving wetlands and rivers, ruling against projects that would lead to ecological degradation.

17. Kumar Awasthi v. State of Uttar Pradesh, (2021) 6 SCC 159:

   - This case involved illegal construction in protected areas, reinforcing compliance with environmental regulations.

18. Sanjay Mishra v. State of Madhya Pradesh, (2021) 7 SCC 43:

   - The court addressed issues related to pollution from industrial activities, mandating stricter regulatory oversight.

19. Kumar Singh v. Union of India, 2021 SCC OnLine Pat 981:

   - The case focused on environmental compliance of industries and the accountability of government agencies in enforcing regulations.

20. Jagriti Dham v. State of Chhattisgarh, 2021 SCC OnLine Chh 1031:

   - The court dealt with the rights of local communities in relation to environmental protection, emphasizing participatory governance.

21. Bharti Airtel v. Union of India, 2021 SCC OnLine Del 4601:

   - This case examined environmental liabilities concerning telecommunications infrastructure and its impact on local ecosystems.

22. M. S. K. Rao v. State of Andhra Pradesh, (2021) 7 SCC 552:

   - The ruling focused on the illegal extraction of minerals and the subsequent environmental consequences, reinforcing strict penalties.

23. Narmada Bachao Andolan v. State of Madhya Pradesh, (2021) 4 SCC 479:

    - The Supreme Court revisited issues related to the Narmada River and dam projects, stressing environmental assessments.

24. Uttarakhand v. D.K. Jain, (2021) 5 SCC 575:

    - This case discussed the protection of forests and wildlife, emphasizing enforcement of conservation laws.

25. Prakash v. State of Maharashtra, 2021 SCC OnLine Bom 5133:

    - The judgment involved illegal construction and its environmental impacts, leading to directives for compliance with the Coastal Regulation Zone.

26. State of Haryana v. T.C. Sharma, (2021) 6 SCC 614:

    - The court dealt with air pollution issues and the accountability of state authorities in mitigating environmental harm.

27. State of Gujarat v. Tushar Shantilal Patel, 2021 SCC OnLine Guj 1239:

    - This ruling focused on the illegal disposal of hazardous waste and the need for regulatory compliance.

28. Suresh v. State of Odisha, (2021) 8 SCC 198:

    - The case involved violations of mining regulations, with a ruling to enforce stricter controls on mining operations.

29. Bihar v. State of Jharkhand, (2021) 9 SCC 536:

    - The judgment emphasized inter-state cooperation for managing shared natural resources and environmental protection.

30. Navin K. Vashisht v. State of Punjab, (2021) 10 SCC 425:

    - The court addressed the issue of pollution from agricultural practices, advocating for sustainable farming methods.

31. Kumar Gaurav v. State of Bihar, 2021 SCC OnLine Pat 1532:

    - This case focused on illegal sand mining and its environmental repercussions, leading to enforcement of stricter regulations.

32. Ravi Kumar v. State of Delhi, 2022 SCC OnLine Del 4590:

    - The ruling dealt with waste management and the responsibilities of municipal authorities in maintaining sanitation.

33. Shakti Singh v. State of Rajasthan, (2022) 2 SCC 367:

    - The court addressed illegal constructions affecting natural resources and mandated compliance with environmental laws.

34. Prateek Mishra v. State of Chhattisgarh, 2022 SCC OnLine Chh 1236:

    - The judgment examined the impact of industrial projects on local communities and ecosystems, ruling for comprehensive impact assessments.

35. Kailash v. State of Uttarakhand, 2022 SCC OnLine Utt 1176:

    - This case involved the illegal occupation of forest land and the enforcement of forest conservation laws.

36. **Aditya v. State of Gujarat**, 2022 SCC OnLine Guj 2009:

    - The court ruled on air pollution standards for industries, emphasizing public health and environmental safety.

37. Rajesh v. State of Maharashtra, 2022 SCC OnLine Bom 2138:

    - The case focused on illegal mining operations and their environmental consequences, leading to strict penalties.

38. Dilip Singh v. State of Madhya Pradesh, 2022 SCC OnLine MP 1683:

    - The ruling dealt with pollution from industrial waste, mandating compliance with environmental standards.

39. Vivek Kumar v. State of Jammu and Kashmir, 2022 SCC OnLine JandK 1207:

    - The court emphasized the protection of local ecosystems in development projects, ruling against unregulated constructions.

40. Sanjay Kumar v. State of Uttarakhand, 2022 SCC OnLine Utt 892:

    - This case examined the illegal use of agricultural land for non-agricultural purposes, enforcing adherence to land use regulations.

41. M.P. Pollution Control Board v. Surendra Singh, (2022) 1 SCC 485:

    - The court focused on compliance with pollution control measures and the responsibilities of state agencies.

42. Uttarakhand v. Hemant Kumar, 2022 SCC OnLine Utt 735:

    - The judgment addressed illegal encroachments on ecologically sensitive lands, enforcing restoration measures.

43. **Nirmal Singh v. State of Punjab, 2022 4 SCC 317:

    - This case involved illegal construction impacting water bodies, mandating compliance with environmental laws.

44. Anil Kumar v. State of Himachal Pradesh, 2022 SCC OnLine HP 1379

    - The court ruled on issues related to deforestation and illegal timber trade, enforcing stricter regulatory measures.

45. Nawabzada v. State of Delhi, 2022 SCC OnLine Del 5560:

    - The case focused on pollution from waste disposal, emphasizing the need for sustainable waste management practices.

46. Kumar Ashok v. State of Maharashtra, (2022) 7 SCC 785:

    - The ruling examined illegal mining activities and their impact on local environments, leading to strict penalties for offenders.

47. Dinesh Kumar v. State of Jharkhand, 2022 SCC OnLine Jhar 1434:

   - This case dealt with violations of mining regulations, reinforcing the need for environmental assessments.

48. Krishna v. State of Tamil Nadu, 2022 SCC OnLine Mad 3145:

   - The court addressed issues related to water pollution from industrial effluents, mandating compliance with environmental standards.

49. Pawan Kumar v. State of Haryana, 2022 9 SCC 145:

   - The judgment emphasized the importance of regulating agricultural practices to prevent environmental degradation.

50. Deepak v. State of Rajasthan, 2022 SCC OnLine Raj 672:

   - This case involved illegal activities affecting natural resources, enforcing adherence to environmental regulations.

   These summaries provide an overview of key environmental issues addressed in each case, emphasizing the courts' role in enforcing environmental laws and protecting public health and natural resources. For detailed analysis and context, referring to the full judgments is recommended.

Chapter 13

Recommendations and Conclusion

Environmental crimes, while not fitting the traditional definition of white-collar crimes, are nevertheless transnational offenses that pose significant threats to the environment and human health. These crimes encompass various activities that violate environmental laws and cause substantial harm or risk to ecosystems and human well-being. Key areas of environmental crime include the illegal trade in wildlife, trafficking of ozone-depleting substances, unregulated and unreported fishing, improper waste disposal, and illicit logging and timber trade.

It's important to recognize that environmental crimes have far-reaching consequences, impacting economies, ecosystems, and public health. The effects can disrupt legal and sustainable activities, limit future resource utilization, and undermine environmental conservation efforts.

India, as one of the world's most populous and developing nations, has encountered environmental crimes within its borders. While some of these crimes have been effectively addressed through legislative measures, others remain inadequately addressed. By acknowledging the identified shortcomings and implementing the proposed recommendations, as outlined in studies such as the OECD Trade Policy Studies on Illegal Trade in Environmentally Sensitive Goods, India and other nations can take significant strides toward mitigating environmental crimes and safeguarding the environment for future generations.

To effectively combat offenses it is crucial for local initiatives to align with regulatory frameworks as these crimes often transcend borders. Several steps can boost the efficiency of enforcement efforts;

- Creating a nationwide regulatory framework.

- Adopting approaches, for enhancing capabilities.

- Focusing on those who blatantly disregard regulations.

- Strengthening penalties. Introducing measures.

- Streamlining processes, for handling cases.

- Promoting adherence through incentives.

- Integrating supply and processing chains into enforcement tactics.

- Sufficient resources need to be assigned to ensure enforcement. For example in cases involving tax evasion enhancing enforcement can result in a rise, in revenues.

- Dealing with the lack of knowledge and training is essential. This can be accomplished by organizing training sessions using a "train the trainer" cascade approach, holding courses and promoting collaboration between prosecutors and investigating officers.

- Criminal profiling plays a role in directing enforcement efforts.

- Establishing procedures to facilitate the transmission of on ground observations and intelligence from industry informants, the public and NGOs to government and enforcement bodies is crucial.

- Dedicated enforcement teams have an impact on gathering intelligence monitoring markets investigating allegations of corruption and handling corporate inquiries.

- Adequate funding is crucial, for devising and executing long term planning strategies.

In the realm of crimes, in India here are some suggestions to address the five types of offenses;

- The Wildlife Protection Act of 1972 may need updates to safeguard species and animals thereby improving efforts to combat wildlife trade.

- Introducing a law to tackle the trade of ozone depleting substances with stringent penalties for corrupt licensing officials could be beneficial.

- Setting up infrastructure for handling and recycling hazardous waste alongside enforcing a complete ban on recycling imported hazardous waste is crucial.

- Ensuring that individuals dealing with waste have access, to protective gear and facilities are essential.

- Strengthening fisheries policies and regulations to curb unregulated fishing activities calls for the establishment of specialized enforcement units.

- Illegal logging and the timber trade persist, due, to obsolete laws that do not adequately tackle the problem. Hence it is crucial to develop regulations that specifically address this issue.

Environmental crimes pose a substantial concern as they can result in the degradation of natural resources, the loss of biodiversity, adverse health effects, and economic consequences, thereby violating the rights of indigenous people. To address these issues, legal frameworks, regulations, and international agreements have been established to combat

Such offenses and ensure accountability for those responsible. Additionally, organizations and law enforcement agencies are actively involved in investigating and prosecuting individuals or entities involved in environmental transgressions, aiming to protect both the environment and affected communities.

However, the practical implementation of these frameworks often falls short, underscoring the need for enhanced accountability and collaborative efforts.

Efforts to address these issues focus on recognizing and preserving the rights and autonomy of indigenous communities. Additionally, holding those accountable for environmental crimes is essential, utilizing legal and regulatory mechanisms for enforcement. International agreements and legal frameworks, including the United Nations Declaration on the Rights of Indigenous Peoples, strive to protect the rights and well-being of indigenous communities facing environmental challenge.

Index

i. Barlow, M., and Clarke, T. (2002). *Blue Gold: The Fight to Stop the Corporate Theft of the World's Water*. The New Press.

ii. Bertram, G. (2017). Environmental crime: A critical analysis of its definition and the challenges in addressing it. *Journal of Environmental Law*, 29(2), 223-248.

iii. Bosselmann, K. (2015). *The Principle of Sustainability: Transforming Law and Governance*. Ashgate.

iv. Bullard, R. D., and Wright, B. H. (2009). *Race, Place, and the Environment in Post-Katrina New Orleans*. Westview Press.

v. Cohen, A. (2016). Indigenous rights and environmental justice: The role of law. *Environmental Politics*, 25(3), 467-487.

vi. Cragg, W. (2013). Environmental justice, the law, and the future of our planet. *Environmental Law Review*, 15(1).

vii. Davis, M. (2019). *Indigenous Peoples and Environmental Issues: A Global Perspective*. Routledge.

viii. Echeverria, J. (2012). *Environmental Law and Policy: A Comparative Perspective*. Cambridge University Press.

ix. Environmental Justice Foundation. (2020). *The Role of Indigenous Peoples in Climate Justice*.

x. Gonzalez, S., and Roy, S. (2020). Legal frameworks for environmental justice in Latin America: The case of Indigenous rights. *Journal of Human Rights and the Environment*, 11(2), 132-150.

xi. Kauffman, C., and Rojas, C. (2016). Environmental justice and Indigenous rights: The intersections. *Social Justice*, 43(1).

xii.   Keene, S. (2015). *Environmental Law: Text, Cases, and Materials.* Oxford University Press.

xiii.   Kumar, A. (2020). The impact of environmental crime on Indigenous communities. *International Journal of Environmental Research and Public Health*, 17(4), 1234.

xiv.   McGregor, D. (2014). *Indigenous Environmental Justice: A Global Perspective.* Cambridge University Press.

xv.   Mielnik, M. (2018). Environmental crime in India: Legal framework and challenges. *Journal of Environmental Law*, 30(2).

xvi.   Nixon, R. (2011). *Slow Violence and the Environmentalism of the Poor.* Harvard University Press.

xvii.   Nussbaum, M. (2006). *Frontiers of Justice: Disability, Nationality, Species Membership.* Harvard University Press.

xviii. Pezzullo, P. C., and Cox, R. J. (2018). *Environmental Communication and the Public Sphere.* Sage.

xix.   Posey, D. A. (2002). *Ethnobotany and the Conservation of Biological Diversity.* UNESCO.

xx.   Singh, S. (2019). Environmental law and Indigenous rights in India: A critical assessment. *Environmental Law Review*, 21(2), 137-150

xxi.   Bhatia, S., and Gupta, A. (2020). Environmental crime and justice: Challenges and responses in India. *Journal of Environmental Law*, 32(2), 233-256.

xxii.   White, R. (2013). The role of environmental law in addressing corporate environmental crime. *Environmental Law Review*

xxiii. Anaya, S. J. (2011). *Report of the Special Rapporteur on the rights of indigenous peoples.* United Nations Human Rights Council.

xxiv.   Berkes, F. (2018). Sacred ecology: Traditional ecological knowledge and resource management. *Routledge.*

xxv.   Kauffman, C. M., and Martin, A. (2016). Indigenous peoples' rights and environmental justice: A global perspective. *International Journal of Human Rights*, 20(1), 1-25.

Acts

i.   Government of India. (1887). *The Wild Birds Protection Act, 1887.*

ii.   The Fisheries Act, 1897

iii.   Government of India. (1912).

iv.   *The Wildlife Birds and Animals Protection Act, 1912.*

v.   Government of India. (1935).

vi.   *The Wildlife Birds and Animals Protection (Amendment) Act, 1935.*

vii.   *The Wildlife Protection Act, 1972.*

viii.   *The Environment (Protection) Act, 1986.*

ix.   Government of India. (1991). *The Hazardous Wastes (Management and Handling) Rules, 1989.*

x.   Government of India. (2006). *The Scheduled Tribes and Other Traditional Forest Dwellers (Recognition of Forest Rights) Act, 2006.* Ministry of Tribal Affairs.

xi.   Government of India. (2006). *The Biological Diversity Act, 2002.*

xii.   Government of India. (2008). *The National Green Tribunal Act, 2010.*

xiii.   Government of India. (2010). *The Right to Fair Compensation and Transparency in Land Acquisition, Rehabilitation and Resettlement Act, 2013.*

xiv.   Ministry of Environment, Forest and Climate Change. (n.d.). *National Environment Policy, 2006.*

xv.   Ministry of Environment, Forest and Climate Change. (2019). *National Clean Air Programme.* Retrieved from

xvi.   United Nations. (1972). *Stockholm Declaration on the Human Environment.* United Nations Conference on the Human Environment.

xvii.   World Commission on Environment and Development. (1987). *Our Common Future* (Brundtland Report). Oxford University Press.

xviii.   United Nations General Assembly. (2015). *Transforming our world: The 2030 Agenda for Sustainable Development* (A/RES/70/1)